THE DOG REDEEMERS

FINDING FOREVER HOMES

A COMPREHENSIVE GUIDE TO DOG RESCUE AND TRAINING

John Kalevi Sievila

Outskirts Press, Inc.
Denver, Colorado

The opinions expressed in this manuscript are solely the opinions of the author and do not represent the opinions or thoughts of the publisher. The author represents and warrants that s/he either owns or has the legal right to publish all material in this book.

The Dog Redeemers
Finding Forever Homes
A Comprehensive Guide to Dog Rescue and Training
All Rights Reserved
Copyright © 2006 John Kalevi Sievila

This book may not be reproduced, transmitted, or stored in whole or in part by any means, including graphic, electronic, or mechanical without the express written consent of the publisher except in the case of brief quotations embodied in critical articles and reviews.

Outskirts Press
http://www.outskirtspress.com

ISBN-10: 1-59800-485-9
ISBN-13: 978-1-59800-485-4

Copyright © 2006 *John Kalevi Sievila*. All rights reserved.

No part of this publication may be reproduced, stored in a retrieval system or transmitted in any form or by any means, electronic, mechanical, photocopying, recording, scanning or otherwise, except as permitted under Sections 107 or 108 of the 1976 United States Copyright Act, without written permission.

Outskirts Press and the "OP" logo are trademarks belonging to
Outskirts Press, Inc.

Printed in the United States of America

A WORD OF CAUTION

Sufficiently provoked any dog will bite. Breeding, personality, and temperament are contributing factors in aggression, but not sole determiners. Exercise caution when handling aggressive dogs, especially larger and athletic breeds. Once a dog has been treated for aggression there are no guarantees that it won't resurface. The techniques outlined in this book will help to minimize and control aggressive tendencies. If you have safety concerns seek the help of a professional.

DEDICATION

This book is dedicated to all the canine rescue organizations and their volunteers who contribute countless hours of tireless work towards the rescue, rehabilitation, and placement of unwanted canines.

ACKNOWLEDGEMENTS

I would like to express my gratitude to Arizona Beagle Rescue, BoxerLuv Rescue, Ashen K-9 Academy and Pets Are People Too for their cooperation.

My sincere thanks to the following for their contributions: to my lovely wife Danette whose constant encouragement made this book a reality. To J. Michael, Karen Ann, and Helen for their creative input and energy.

TABLE OF CONTENTS

INTRODUCTION	i
BENEVOLENT LEADERSHIP	1
Case Study: High Anxiety	2
THE DEN	5
Case Study: Kennel Craze	7
Case Study: The Great Escape	9
FEEDING	12
Case Study: My Dog is Starving!	14
Case Study: Food Fight!	16
THE WALK	19
Case Study: The Dog that Pulled Too Hard	22
Case Study: The Door Dasher	24
SPEAKING A DOG'S LANGUAGE	27
Case Study: Jumpin Gehosafat	30
Case Study: In Your Face	32
HOUSEBREAKING	34
Case Study: The Accidental Canine	37
Case Study: Pissing Contest	38
BARKING	41
Case Study: Excessive Barking	43
Case Study: The Invisible Perpetrator	45
POSSESSIONS	48
Case Study: Bite the Hand that Feeds	50
Case Study: Trophies	52

BONDING	55
Case Study: What Have You Done to My Kid?	56
Case Study: Jekyll and Hyde	58
AGRESSION	62
Case Study: The Reluctant Defender	67
Case Study: The Bully Pulpit	69
PUPPY IMPRINTING	73
Case Study: Driving Ms. Daisy	75
Case Study: Unforgivable	78
BASIC OBEDIENCE	81
Training Lesson 1	84
Training Lesson 2	85
Training Lesson 3	86
Training Lesson 4	87
Program Guidelines Do(s) & Don't(s)	88
Establishing Alpha	90

INTRODUCTION

Having worked on the rehabilitation of hundreds of rescued dogs over the past 10 years, I've witnessed firsthand the insensitivity and cruelty people can bestow on man's best friend. Mankind has concocted all sorts of damning exercises for these animals, from puppy mills where dogs spend their entire lives in a small confined space highlighted by presenting several litters a year to dogs bred for the sole purpose of fighting. In the end I am always amazed at the resiliency and grace these amazing animals extend toward us, their benevolent masters.

Combating insensitivity and cruelty is a worthy endeavor and over the years several canine rescue groups have been organized to rescue and rehabilitate these abused and neglected dogs. Sadly much too often, rescue groups are called to rescue and rehabilitate these dogs from very dire circumstances. It seems that on a weekly basis we receive news reports on puppy mills and dog fighting rings broken up with abused dogs dispatched to local rescue groups which represents only a small portion of the dogs that are rescued. Of the thousands of calls rescue groups receive each day, a majority are owners requesting to turn in their dogs due to unwanted or bad behavior. Reasons vary from soiling inside the house, to *"... we have a new baby in the house and just don't have the time"*, or in some cases expressions of aggression directed toward owners and/or family members. When irresponsible pet owners turn in their family dogs they are simply passing the problem onto the rescue groups. Rescue groups in most cases are non-profit organizations working with limited resources and funding, relying on volunteers to do the majority of the work. Rescue groups don't have the time or resources to hire professional trainers or behaviorists to fix the problems of the multitude of dogs they receive. Bottom line, dog owners need to take responsibility and do the right thing in getting help for their dogs instead of relying on rescue groups to solve their problem.

It's been said, "...that there is no such thing as a bad dog, just a bad owner." There is some truth to that statement, however; reality is ignorant dog owners create badly behaved dogs. It has been my experience that 99% of all bad behavior can be controlled with the correct techniques. In only rare cases where a dog is "hardwired" wrong that behavior cannot be modified. Of the hundreds of rescue dogs I have worked with only a half dozen or so could not be rehabilitated. That said, one truth remains; 100% of all bad behavior can be traced back to one common element: *The lack of benevolent leadership and control in the household.*

When called out to evaluate a "problem" dog, it is always the result of some sort of "climactic" event such as tearing a living room apart or a bad dog bite. The problem rarely started with the climactic event itself but was merely the logical conclusion to a series of behaviors that were allowed to go "unchecked." Through no intentional fault of their own, the owners' ignorance has left the dog thinking that it is in charge. In their minds the home is their "den" and as such they are allowed to do whatever they want, whenever they want. In their way of thinking how dare we try to correct them for any behavior in their domain. This is a daunting problem and difficult attitude to correct, but with diligent work we can effect a change for the better.

The information presented in this book is intended to provide a method for understanding how and why our dogs interact with us the way they do. Understanding how our dogs see us, gauging our interactions and systematically responding to them we will be able to establish and maintain our role as benevolent leaders within our households and ultimately have a happy, confident, and well contented life long family member in our canine.

CHAPTER I
BENEVOLENT LEADERSHIP
THE MASTER'S WISHES

Domesticated dogs' ancestry can be traced back to the wolf. It has been noted that all domesticated dogs are only five generations removed from the wild. The wolf has survived millennia under a canine social structure known as "the Pack." It is the study of the wolf pack that has created several successful methods for analyzing, understanding, and modifying domestic dog behavior.

Utmost and foremost within the pack hierarchy are the leaders known as the "Alpha Pair." The Alpha Pair eats first, only ones who mate, dictate access to the den, and make every important decision for the Pack. They initiate scouting missions, determine hunting grounds, and lead the hunt. The survival of the Pack is predicated on the Alphas' ability to accomplish these tasks. For the Pack they are the center of the universe and their desires, pleasures, and will paramount.

Preservation of the Pack is an overriding instinct for all dogs. In order for a Pack to survive and prosper it must have strong leadership. Domesticated dogs being highly social adapt well into the structure of the human family. They see their owners and other family members as part of the Pack. Without clear leadership present any dog will assume the Alpha role. In their minds having Pack leadership is paramount; anything less and the Pack would breakdown in chaos and be destroyed.

Our domesticated dogs are ill equipped to be Alpha leaders of a human family, let alone a wild wolf pack. It would be the equivalent of a

12-year old boy or girl trying to drive to school, hold down a full time job, and pay the mortgage. Placing our dog in the Alpha role leads to anxiety, bad behavior, and in some cases down right aggression.

Make no mistake; Alphas (both dog and human) are dominant and sometimes cruel dictators. Their tool is domination with the goal of imposing their will and pleasure on the pack and its' members. Common scenes of cruelty play out everyday in the form of wild dog-on-dog bloodletting or humans beating dogs showcasing our nature at its worst. As humans it is asserting our dominance and imposing our will, while removing the cruelty that transforms us into benevolent leaders.

The key characteristics to strong benevolent leadership are *Calm, Confidence, and Consistency*. Effective benevolent leaders radiate a calm quiet confidence when interacting with their subordinates. This is especially important when we interact with our dogs. At home when we raise our voices, argue, play loudly, or otherwise act out emotions we tend to confuse and frustrate our dogs. Keep in mind that dogs don't understand human language but can recognize words; they associate sound and our body posture as their form of communication. As humans we communicate ninety five percent verbally and five percent with body language. With dogs it is the exact opposite. The way we posture or otherwise position our bodies' sends very strong signals to dogs. Without understanding this hidden language we can unknowingly send confusing messages to our dogs. Add to that inconsistency, it's no wonder our dogs think that they have to assume the leadership position within the pack. The first sign of trouble is usually a form of anxiety.

CASE STUDY: HIGH ANXIETY

One of the worst cases of anxiety I've encountered was some years ago in the Mid-west; it involved a lovely two-year-old petite sheltie named "Sandy". The local veterinarian had adopted her and while away from home during the day had hired a neighbor to take care of her. One of the first things the neighbor noticed was that when she entered the home Sandy would run and hide. After a few minutes the neighbor would be able to corral the dog and take her on lead into her unfenced backyard. Once in the backyard even more distressing was whenever any noise was present either from a school bus or an airplane she would become absolutely frantic to the point of urinating and purging her anal glands. The neighbor did what most people would do and that was to calm the dog down by telling her everything was going to be all right. To make matters worse whenever there was a thunderstorm the petite sheltie would try to break through windows to get away from what she thought was impending doom. Being a good veterinarian and responsible pet owner, the good doctor promptly prescribed tranquilizers for Sandy to be taken in the event of an impending thunderstorm. Not knowing the complete history of this rescued dog there must have been some traumatic experience that led to this behavior.

One would think that this dog was simply abused in some manner and that this sort of behavior was something that would have to be tolerated for the next twelve to fourteen years of Sandy's life. Not only is this untrue, but the conclusion unacceptable.

The underlying problem was the lack of a perceived Alpha Pair. The symptom manifested was severe anxiety over noise. Sandy had been forced to accept the role of Alpha in this human household (or "Pack") of two adults and two children. Despite being a veterinarian the family had unknowingly done just about everything wrong. They had been sending the wrong signals about who was in charge, starting with the dog's sleeping location, daily feeding routine, and correcting of bad behavior. To make matters worse whenever Sandy showed any anxiety or fear they would coddle her by acknowledging the threat by telling her, "… everything would be all right". This works for humans because we understand language, but for dogs it is just sounds like "… blah, blah, blah…" and in their minds it just acknowledges that there is something to be fearful of.

Most types of bad behavior do not need to be addressed directly but are simply resolved once a benevolent Alpha is established as leader of the Pack. In this case however, not only did there need to be benevolent leadership established, but the anxiety of noise had to be dealt with directly. We spent the first few weeks-establishing benevolent Alpha leadership (covered in detail in this book), and then dealt directly with the noise. We needed to wait for a good old-fashioned Midwestern thunderstorm to take the next step.

One of the techniques we have used successfully with high anxiety dogs is what we call affectionately the "Umbilical cord". We simply attach one end of a 6-foot lead to the dog and the other end to our belt loop. This requires the dog to go where we go; the key is to simply ignore the dog until it is time to remove the lead. This teaches the dog that whatever it fears has no consequence to us as Alpha leaders and in fact we don't even acknowledge their perceived threat. Doing so sends the signal to the dog that this is nothing to fear and in the long run builds their confidence.

Now back to Sandy and the thunderstorm. We attached the "Umbilical Cord" to Sandy and proceeded to work outside (in a protected area) with absolutely no acknowledgement whatsoever of the passing thunderstorm storm. One can only imagine what was going through Sandy' mind. She must of thought, "… what is wrong with this guy and why is he not heading for cover, doesn't he know we are about to be destroyed …". It was a struggle and took several storms but with benevolent Alpha leadership personifying a quiet confidence, a strong non-verbal communication, and a steadfast consistency, Sandy no longer needs medication and remains calm during thunderstorms.

CHAPTER 2
THE DEN

A CHANGING OF THE GUARD

One of the most important items to consider when establishing Alpha is the den. As far as our dogs are concerned they view our home as the pack's den and as far as their line of sight the pack's territory. How we grant access to space in the den sends a very strong message as to the dogs' status in the pack. Remember Alphas can come and go as they please with access to any part of the den they choose, in their mind it's their den.

One of the first questions to ask during an evaluation is "where does the dog sleep at night?" Inevitably the answer is either on the bed, bedroom floor, or another part of the house. The next question is," Is the bedroom door open?" Usually the answer is "Yes" and the point needs to be made diplomatically that the dog sleeps wherever it wants to because it has free roam of the den. It simply chooses to sleep in the bedroom because it wants to monitor its Pack members. Most people get the message and start to realign their thinking with the dogs. Sleep location sends an incredibly strong message to the dog of its status in the pack. Dogs that are allowed to sleep on the bed with us sends the message that they are high ranking members of the pack or perhaps even Alpha.

To reset the "Den" message and set the dogs' new expectation, the first order of business is to introduce the dog to a kennel. Dogs are natural den-ing animals and will find a kennel location in the den whether it is provided for or not, such as under a coffee table, in a corner, or underneath our bed covers. I will make a strong point here, "Kenneling or crating a dog does not cause harm". The key point to remember is that placing the dog in the kennel is never to be used as a form of punishment or other negative experience. The kennel is the dog's refuge and should always be used as a positive experience.

To kennel train a dog you must begin by getting the dog to go into the kennel with as minimum physical force from you as possible. You're probably wondering how in the heck that is done with a dog that doesn't want to go into the kennel to begin with. Very simple, position the dog in front of the open kennel, if the dog moves right or left, reposition him/her in front of the open kennel door. Remove the option of not entering the open kennel. Avoid physically pushing the dog (with hands) into the kennel; once your dog enters give him/her plenty of praise and affection. This is the only time that we encourage with a treat as a reward for entering the kennel; this makes it an extremely positive experience.

If your dog is having trouble entering the open kennel, it's ok to place the treat inside so the dog goes in after it. Again close the door behind the canine and heap lots of praise and affection (positive reinforcement).

The next step is absolutely crucial. If the dog starts to show signs of anxiety completely ignore the behavior. Any form of verbal, physical or eye contact during the drama will only add to the anxiety. Never yell at the dog to shut-up or coddle them in any way. Even if the dog appears to be hell bent on destroying the kennel, ignore the behavior. The next thing you will do is leave the room for a few minutes (10 minutes or more) making sure that you're out of ear shot, eye sight, and smell range. One key concept to remember is that dogs live in the "here and now", beyond 5-10 minutes they don't have the concept of the passage of time, so when you return they don't know exactly how long you've been gone. They don't know if you've been gone 5 minutes, 5 hours, or 5 days. From their prospective they only realize that you've left the room and you've returned. It is important that upon return you ignore the dog completely, until the canine has been calm for a minimum of 5 minutes (known as the "5 minute rule"). It is important not to let them out immediately; doing so sends them a strong message that they are a high-ranking member of the pack. Now we can prepare to let them out of the kennel. That's right "prepare," that doesn't mean to simply open the kennel door and let them dart out.

Prior to letting them out of the kennel (or crate) you must impose the concept of "Threshold Respect", meaning that when you open the kennel door if the dog tries to bolt out, you will simply close the kennel door on the dog's nose. You will continue to open and close the door until the dog remains stationary and you say the magic word "ok" allowing them to exit the kennel into the den. This sends an extremely strong message that you are the Alpha and that you dictate who has access to the den.

When you first begin kennel training you'll want to repeat this exercise 2-3 times daily. This will remove any anxiety the dog may have. What the dog learns is that entering the kennel is a positive experience, under all circumstances they won't be stranded in the kennel, and as an Alpha you will return to let them out.

At nighttime during the "boot camp" period (first 12 weeks) the dog will be required to sleep in the kennel overnight. In some cases owners have complained that', "… the first few nights the dog kept me up all night whining". What I've recommended in the past and has worked well is its ok to put the kennel in your locked car in the garage providing it is not to cold or hot at night. This way the noise is muffled, you get your sleep and after 2 or 3 nights your dog has overcome any anxiety over being kenneled. Remember the keys: calm, confidence, and consistency will get you through this process.

Now the kenneling does not have to be permanent. In most cases after 12 weeks owners can remove the kennel door giving the dog the option to sleep in or out of the kennel. What is interesting is that in a majority of cases the dog will choose to sleep in the kennel because it feels safe and protected.

CASE STUDY: KENNEL CRAZE

Aptly named, "Separation Anxiety", can manifest itself in many forms and one of the most destructive and potentially dangerous to the dog is called "Kennel Craze". Separation anxiety is not what most people think. Most often dog owners incorrectly characterize it as their dog is acting out because he or she somehow misses them. In reality, the dog is not acting out because it is somehow longing for its' owners but rather is reacting out of stress associated with their Alpha responsibilities. Consider this, if you were locked in your home and thought that your 2 and 3 year olds had wandered outside and somehow wound up playing on the freeway, you would be absolutely frantic. In your dog's mind they're in charge, you're one of their pack members, and therefore they are responsible for your well being. How dare you leave the house without them in tow. Every time you leave them alone in the house, you've left them to go play on the freeway or so your dog would think. That mindset explains quite a bit when you consider the destructive behavior separation anxiety episodes can initiate.

I recently received a call from a local Dachshund Rescue group that had gotten a owner surrender call for a eleven pound, four year old Dachshund named "Scotty". Scotty was a holy terror on four legs. The owners had explained that the dog had such severe separation anxiety that it would completely destroy the house anytime the owners left. They had tried over the years to kennel the dog without success. This last time when they had tried to kennel the dog, Scotty had chewed his way out of a plastic dog kennel losing a couple of teeth and leaving a significant blood trail behind in the process.

The owners were completely beside themselves. They simply adored their Scotty giving him all the accolades and consideration due royalty, basically responding to every demand and letting Scotty do just about anything he wanted too. From a pup, Scotty had been allowed to sleep in bed with the owners, allowed to free feed during the day, and was given his way if he raised his lips or growled, all strong signals that Scotty was a high-ranking member of the pack. Clearly in Scotty's mind he was in charge.

Over the years they had gotten much of the same bad advice most dog owners get. They had been told by their vet to put blankets in the kennel that had their scent on it. This would somehow make Scotty feel close to them while they were away. It doesn't take a genius to guess what happened next; upon entry into newly adorned kennel Scotty promptly ripped the blankets into shreds. Don't get me wrong, most veterinarians are great about taking care of canine's physical ailments, but some miss the mark when it comes to modifying a dog's behavior. It like the old adage, "… a mechanic's car never runs right or … a doctor's' kids are always sick …". Naturally it goes without saying that in some cases veterinarian's dogs are the worst behaved.

To underscore the point, the next suggestion from the veterinarian was to get a puppy to keep Scotty company. Somehow this was supposed to calm Scotty down and eliminate the separation anxiety. It's been said, " … that having two dogs is half the work of having one", but I can tell you from experience it doesn't fix separation anxiety and usually only compounds the problem. The owners quit taking their veterinarians behavioral advice when prescribed tranquilizers didn't stop Scotty's anxiety.

Separation Anxiety was just a symptom of the root cause, which was that Scotty had accepted the role of Alpha for this household ("Pack") and all the responsibilities associated with it. Adding the puppy to the mix only added to Scotty's responsibility and anxiety. The first step in correcting Scotty's behavior was to reset his status within the pack to a subordinate member. This took some effort on part of the owners, but after a few weeks of diligently following the program guidelines and reinforcing it with basic obedience training Scotty no longer has any issues when it comes time to being left home alone in the kennel.

CASE STUDY: THE GREAT ESCAPE

Growing up we had a family dog named "Rickey". Rickey was a Dalmatian Pit Bull Mix, an excellent family dog that never displayed any aggression towards anyone. Every dog has its issues and in Rickey's case he loved to jump fences. Once free from the confines of the backyard Rickey would venture out to look for other dogs. No matter how hard we would chase him or call his name, he always would stay just out of reach and after a couple of hours would return home.

On several occasions Rickey would return bloody and worn from an obvious dogfight. The one and only time we witnessed the bloodletting Rickey had clearly been the aggressor. Finally my father had had enough and decided to erect a cable with an attaching chain that Rickey could maneuver around with. It seemed like a pretty good idea at the time and gave Rickey about 80 feet of room. This worked for a while until one afternoon I went out to the backyard to find the chain had looped over the fence and caught between two boards. My first thought was that Rickey had snapped the chain and was out on the run again. To my horror, I looked over the fence to see Rickey dead from a broken neck. I was fourteen years old at the time and to this day that image still haunts me.

It is one of the reasons that I began to work with rescue groups. I wanted to understand why dogs behave the way they do and find ways to modify unwanted or bad behavior. To this day one of top challenges is preventing escapes. Anytime a dog escapes from the back yard, it's a serious issue. We've all heard the stories about dogs that get out of their yards only to get hit by a car or worse. Recently I had the opportunity of working with a 13-year-old Border Collie named "Bucky" who would on a daily basis perform what I called "The Great Escape".

Bucky's owners had recently moved back in with the Son's parents. It is tough anytime grown kids need to move back in with their parents and can be just as difficult for any pets. In this case the parents didn't want Bucky loose in the house while all were away for the day at school and work. So the thought was to have Bucky stay in the fenced backyard during the day. Bucky had other ideas. Returning back to the household the first day the dog was nowhere to be found. To make matters even more perplexing there was no evidence as to how Bucky escaped.

The owner had made sure that there were no obvious escape routes from the cyclone-fenced backyard. Nonetheless Bucky was nowhere in sight and after several hours of searching Bucky returned from down a nearby bicycle path a little muddy but none the worse for wear. This saga repeated itself for a few days until I received the call to come investigate the problem.

The owner's parents assured me that there was no way Bucky could be getting out on his own and that someone must be letting him out. The owners and the parents argued on about who would do such a thing and that Bucky must have found an opening somewhere in the fence. Tension was so thick you could have sliced it with a knife, surely leading to some anxiety on Bucky's part. I started the evaluation going through the routine steps of identifying the correct sleeping location, proper feeding routine, and basic do's and don'ts. Like most owners they had let Bucky establish himself as Alpha in charge of the Den. In the previous home Bucky had been allowed to come and go via a pet door, a sure sign that in Bucky's mind he was high ranking member of the pack. It was pretty easy to diagnose what was going on here. When his owners left for the day his pack was leaving his Den without his supervision causing a certain level of anxiety. Bucky was simply leaving the backyard to go look for his pack.

Now the mystery was exactly how was Bucky escaping from the backyard? Border Collies are very smart, sometimes smarter then their owners. The owners tried to fool Bucky by pretending they had left the house hoping he would divulge his escape route, to no avail. Eventually we had to setup a video camera and pick certain sections of the fence line to monitor. It took a couple of tries and different angles but to my amazement we caught on video, Bucky a geriatric 13 year-old Border Collie, scaling a 6 foot cyclone-fence to make his escape. Using an electronic collar and providing a stimulus when the dog's front paws hit the fence can usually correct fence jumping. Now the problem was how do you correct this type of behavior with a geriatric dog? An electronic collar in this situation was too much for a dog this age.

Here's the point. Some behaviors cannot be corrected but controlled. It is my firm opinion that when a dog has reached its golden years we should afford them the respect due. You don't put a geriatric dog through any unneeded trauma. Using an electronic collar or any other type of stern correction could cause more damage than good. So the option was clear. Kennel Bucky in the house during the day when the owners were away at work or school. It took some convincing, but the owners finally realized that this was the best thing for Bucky. I am happy to say Bucky lived to the ripe old age of 15 with his last two years being a contented life of leisure as should be for any dog in its golden years.

CHAPTER 3
FEEDING

THERE IS A NEW SHERIFF IN TOWN

The second most important aspect to establishing Alpha is the feeding ritual. In the wild Alphas determine the hunting grounds, initiate the hunt, and begin the feeding. They demonstrate their dominance and impose their will on the pack by eating first and determining who is allowed to eat next. Their dictatorship is absolute, where all signs of mercy shown subordinate pack members are seen as weakness. Food can be a very powerful tool when trying to send a message to our canines. One can imagine what goes on through their minds when they see us dispensing food to them without concern or consequence. Most common mistakes regarding feeding range from feeding the dog table scraps right from the dinner table to leaving food bowls filled at all times allowing the dogs to free feed. Make no mistake, doing so sends the clear message to our dogs that it is their food and we are just here to dispense it to them when they demand it. No wonder so many dogs assume Alpha roles within their households, they're getting their Alpha coronation at feeding time every day.

I don't want to leave you with the wrong impression. Our dogs are truly capable of showing us complete devotion, love, and affection and in turn we reciprocate. It is when we extend mercy rather than affection towards our canines that they see it as a weakness. Weakness in Alphas cannot be tolerated under any circumstances for it will lead to chaos and destruction of the Pack, or so our dogs would think. We absolutely have to insure that when we feed our dogs we are doing it from the Alpha position.

To deliver the message that we are the Alpha and in charge we have to take notice of how we feed our dogs. To begin we must get organized and set a schedule of feeding times for our dogs. Adult dogs need to be fed twice a day; puppies typically need to be fed a minimum of three times a day. The best method I have found for adult dogs is to try to space the morning and late afternoon feeding about ten to eleven hours apart. Ideally a 6:30 AM and 5:30 PM feeding following the dog food company label instructions for the size of your dog is perfect. Feeding the dog at 5:30 PM gives them enough time in the evening to go the bathroom and not have any discomfort during the night that would require your attention. Dogs love structure and consistency, so sticking to the schedule will only reinforce their confidence that you are the Alpha.

At feeding time it is absolutely critical that you follow these guidelines to insure that you are projecting an Alpha status (known as the Alpha feeding technique). When you prepare your dogs food and if they begin to get excited and start posture demanding the food you are to simply ignore them. Once they have been calm for a minimum of 5 minutes you can feed them. The first few times you try this make sure you have enough time to devote to this exercise. You may be spending 30 to 45 minutes getting started. During the food preparation time and whilst you're waiting for the calm, drink and eat something in plain view of your dogs prior to feeding them. Get as many family members involved with this portion of the exercise as possible by eating and drinking in plain view of your dogs. The first time you do this you will not believe the expression you're going to get from your dog. Total shock and possibly horror will be written across their little faces. To quote an old western, "There is a new sheriff in town…"

Equally important to preparation is the manner in which you dispense the food to your dogs. Remember, you're the new sheriff in town and you will decide when your dogs eat and in what order they are allowed to eat. To demonstrate this to your dogs, start to place the dog bowl on the floor if your dog attempts to "Bull rush" it pick up the bowl immediately. Again begin to place the bowl on the floor and if your dogs move forward pick the bowl up. Most likely you'll repeat this exercise a few times emulating a yo-yo before your dog simply remains stationary looking at you in astonishment. Once you have mesmerized your dogs, place the bowl on the floor removing your hands from it and state clearly the magic word "OK!"

Your dogs will do one of two things; either they will start eating or simply turn their backs and walk away. If they choose to walk away they are doing so in defiance and the result will be that you immediately pick up the bowl. If they choose to eat whatever they don't finish in 15 minutes you pick up. Do not leave empty or partially filled dog bowls on the floor. In cases where the dog is choosing not to eat, I will get a call back from the owners lamenting that their dog is going to starve to death. What I diplomatically tell them is that in ten years and hundreds of dogs, we have never had one starve to death. Eventually hunger sets in and the dog will resume eating with usually a better appetite then before. You know that eating someone else's cooking always taste better. Remember the food used to be your dogs, now it is yours and you as Alpha are allowing them to eat according to your dictates.

CASE STUDY: MY DOG IS STARVING!

A common misconception is that our dogs can somehow get upset with us and refuse to eat. The notion is that we should be made to feel guilty by our dog's lack of appetite. This mindset always amazes me and reinforces the point that many people adopt dogs to create a surrogate child relationship. The point is no more self-evident then with the obese canine. Obese canines present a paradox when using food to establish the Alpha in the household. Most often the Alpha feeding exercise presents no problem with overweight dogs; they enjoy food way too much to not fall in line with this exercise. It is the dogs of normal or under weight that can present the most difficulty at feeding time.

Rudy was an abused 2-year-old whippet that had been recently adopted by a family in the Midwest. I received a call from the local rescue group asking that I have discussion with the new owners to determine what the root cause for the lack of eating. In this particular household there was an older established greyhound and two cats that were allowed to roam the house. My first clue that there might be a problem was when I arrived at the house to discover that both dogs where chained to the floor with about two feet of chain they could maneuver about with. Naturally my curiosity immediately got the best of me and I had to ask the question, "Why?"

The owner proudly informed me that greyhounds and whippets are natural hunters and that if they were allowed to run loose they would simply kill the two cats that were allowed to roam free. My first thought was, so you adopted these dogs so that they would be confined to a two by two foot space. Luckily I bit my tongue and started the interview process to determine what could be done to a) get Rudy eating and b) get these two wonderful dogs released from their chains of bondage.

I started the evaluation with the customary question, "Where do the dogs sleep?" Their answer was right there, pointing to the chains. My next question was, "Have you ever tried having them sleep in a kennel?" knowing that the rescue group had provided one with Rudy. The response was that both dogs simply wouldn't be still and tried to break out of the kennels. The first order of business I informed them was that the dogs needed to sleep in the kennel and proceeded to instruct them on kennel training techniques. One issue resolved. Next, why wasn't Rudy eating?

I asked the owners to demonstrate the way they fed the dogs. It was the biggest production since Barnum and Bailey Circus. One adult started by preparing the food on the kitchen counter, which promptly started a chorus of barking from the chained dogs. Imagine this as the backdrop, the other adult in the household was literally chasing, screaming, and corralling the cats to get them segregated into a separate bedroom. Then the real pandemonium broke out, the owners set the dog bowls on the floor and let the dogs off their chains. I never realized a greyhound or whippet could run so fast in a small environment. They were bouncing off the furniture, moving objects about as they flew by all the while for the most part ignoring me and the owners' request to stop. Walt Disney in his prime could not have imagined a better scene of human animal chaos for one of his trademark movies.

Once both dogs calmed down the older greyhound meandered over to his bowl and ate at very slow pace. I watched intently next to see what Rudy would do. He immediately made eye contact with the owner and waited for a response. Getting the owners attention, Rudy then proceeded to walk over to get a drink of water completely ignoring the food. The owner promptly called to Rudy and said, "Come on boy, come and eat for daddy". Showing no interest, the owner set out on the task of hand feeding Rudy and after each bite telling him he was good boy for eating. Naturally, the owners thought they were nursing Rudy back to health. Whippets are naturally thin and from where I was sitting Rudy wasn't going to waste away any time soon.

Obviously these dogs had their owners trained very well. Not only were they getting fed per their wishes, but the owners were complying with just about every demand. When the dogs where loose and demanded to go outside, the owners complied When they were outside if they demanded to come in, the owners complied. If the dogs demanded to be petted, the owners complied. It was as though the guilt of having them chained gave the dog's free license when they were allowed to roam free about the house. I can almost guarantee that under these circumstances that if the cats were allowed out, they would most certainly have become chew toys or much worse. By chaining the dogs to floor, the owners had simply fixed the symptom, but not the problem.

To correct this type of behavior we would have to begin by working on den access. In the wild Alphas dictate who has access to the den. The first important piece to the puzzle would be to insure that the dogs slept in their kennels and be sequestered in their kennels when the owners were away from home. Second item, for the next several weeks the dogs would have to be tethered to an adult at all times via 6 ft lead and chain collar. This technique sets in the dog's mind that the owners are the Alphas and dictate access to the Den.

The next important item was feeding. I absolutely stressed to the owners the importance of following the program feeding guidelines and that without it we would not succeed. I reminded them to follow the steps and that we had never had a dog starve to death as result of following the program. It took about twelve weeks of effort and couple of more visits on my part, but I am happy to report that the dogs no longer need to be chained and are getting along splendidly with the cats.

CASE STUDY: FOOD FIGHT!

I've always been intrigued by other people's perception of the causes and solutions to bad dog behavior. I've spent the better part of my professional career studying root causes of problems and developing processes to correct them. In today's Internet age of emails, websites, and chat rooms it was easy to gather people's perceptions and to exchange ideas with them, especially about dogs. Most local and national rescue organizations have elaborate websites and group email communications where one can readily discuss problems and share solutions.

Recently there was a heated discussion with a national rescue organization email group about in-house dog fighting. The majority of in-house dog fighting centers around food or possession based aggression. Opinions from the email group on causes and solutions varied greatly. Causes ranged from "… my large female is the Alpha and wasn't fed in her spot so …" to " … well tonight they got some special table scraps and something just set them off …" (none of which is a good idea by the way). Solutions vary as well but the one that peaked my interest read something like this, " … I am the Alpha in my household so my dogs always listen to me and when they fight I just let them work it out". This response (and I've seen more than a few times) always floors me. When working with rescue I make this distinct point, "Anytime there is a dog fight in your presence you're not in control nor are you viewed as the Alpha, period." This pronouncement elicits two reactions; complete silence or what can I do to correct this?

Not only is it a very bad idea to " … let them work it out", but it can cause serious injury to the dogs. There is no more tenuous situation then those who foster multiple dogs for local rescue groups. The environment is ever changing due to the constant shuffling of dogs in and out of the home. This is a monumental challenge for the rescue foster homes. This case study centers on a foster home that on most days is fostering eight or nine large Boxers.

Often it is not so much the challenge of setting up a proper environment as it is overcoming myths and misconceptions people have about canines. In this case the foster parents had had many years of experience working with dogs but one main misconception that kenneling dogs was cruel. This conclusion was one of the root causes as to why the dogs were getting into occasional skirmishes at feeding time. Now the trick was convincing the foster parents that kennels (or crates) were not cruel.

Fortunately the foster parents had attended one of our foster in-take seminars at a local pet resort where one comment had resonated with them, " … dogs are naturally "den-ing" animals and will find a kenneling location whether you provide them one or not, such as under a coffee table or in the corner of the room. They like the enclosed space were they feel somewhat protected from attacks from above or behind when they are sleeping." I went on to ask the foster parents if it all made sense why they hadn't been using the kennels and their reply was that it had been so long since they used one they weren't sure how to introduce a new dog to a kennel. I went on to tell them the timing couldn't be better because when the dogs go to their permanent homes they will need to be kenneled at night for the first few weeks and they'll be okay with it because you got them started on the nighttime kenneling.

We immediately established nighttime kenneling with the dogs and moved right into creating this sort of triage for incoming dogs. We decided that the dogs in the home would be divided into two groups, the *short timers* and *long timers*. The short timers were those dogs that had been in the house less then 48 hours. The long timers were those dogs that had been in the house longer then 48 hours. To make sure that there were no fights the rule was to keep short timers separated from the long timers. Upon arrival into the home the short timers would spend the time on the umbilical cord technique (8 foot lead connected to the person's belt loop) when out of the kennel. They would be feed separately using the Alpha feeding technique. At the end of the 48 hour period the dog would be introduced to the long timers gauging whether there would be any dog on dog aggression. If the integration went smoothly then the canine would become part of the long timers group.

Once part of the long timers group the dogs would be fed in groups of 3 or 4 using the Alpha feeding technique with leads attached and dragging on the ground. All bowls of food would be placed on the floor and no one dog would be allowed to move forward to eat until they heard the golden word "OK". There is nothing more impressive then seeing four full grown Boxers sitting stationary in front of full food bowls waiting politely to start eating. If a skirmish broke out the lead would be snatched and the situation brought under control quickly. To make sure there was no sub-hierarchy emerging the groups of three or four would interchange members. This process has worked well in the past and I would highly recommend it to any foster homes housing multiple dogs.

CHAPTER 4
THE WALK
TAKING THE LEAD

There is nothing more serene then a peaceful walk in the great outdoors with one's best friend. For most people this is more of a dream than reality because a majority of dogs lead the walk with their unwilling owners in tow. How many times have you been to the dog park or out in your neighborhood and seen dogs dragging their owners around the block? Worse yet is to witness the emotional confrontation that erupts if another dog or person approaches the procession. Clearly most aggressive tendencies encountered during a walk are caused by two things; one, the owner lacks confidence and shows it; secondly, the dog thinks it is the Alpha and in charge of the walk (hunt). This is never more evident than when an owner looses control of their dog on a walk and an attack occurs. The walk is critical to establishing Alpha status.

In the wild the Alpha pair goes to great measures to prepare pack members for a hunt. The ritual begins by the Alpha pair exciting pack members to a point of controlled frenzy. Once the excitement reaches the desired level the Alpha pair leaves the den and directs the hunt with subordinate pack members in tow.

In comparison note the behavior we see from our dogs when we're at home and ready to take them on their walk. Remove their leashes out of the cupboard and carefully gage their reaction. Naturally most dogs tend to get rather excited, most of the time barely containing themselves while we fumble trying to connect leashes to their collars. The moment the front door opens watch out; almost complete anarchy rushing towards the doorway. All the while our dogs are thinking "... We're going on a Hunt, we're going on a hunt, and we're going on a hunt..."

Each and every time we take our dogs for a walk, we have golden opportunity to either establish or reinforce the Alpha . When I review the process with dog owners they are surprised to hear me tell them that when the leashes come out we are in no way to stifle the dog's excitement. In fact we are to encourage it, just as an Alpha pair would do in the wild. The excitement must be managed to what I call a "Controlled frenzy." What I mean by this is the dogs should be allowed to jump in the air, bounce around, and vocalize to their hearts content. One must draw the line however if the excitement leads to signs of dominance such as jumping on, herding, or blocking the owner. Any actions of this sort must be immediately met with the proper correction (covered later in this book) to insure that the owner is not losing Alpha control.

Once the leashes are on and the dogs are ready to exit the den, the key to sending the first Alpha message is threshold respect. When you get to the front door the dogs are not allowed to enter the threshold until told to do so by a loud "OK". If any of the dogs enter the threshold out of turn promptly hit them (gently, no bruises or broken bones please) with the door to send the message that the threshold is off limits until the Alpha has given the signal. If the dogs continue to crowd the door, gently tap on the top of their paws with the bottom of your shoes letting them know that they better back up.

Once the dogs are under control, ensure that you step out the threshold first. Look back and pause a moment or two and firmly say, "OK" signaling the pack to exit the den. Now that you and the pack have exited the den, as Alpha you must lead the walk. To do so, the dogs cannot pull on their leads. If the dogs pull, apply a correction by snapping the leash sending a strong signal via the chain collar. Yes, that is correct a *Chain Collar*. You should avoid gentle leaders, harnesses, and standard collars when walking your dog for the simple reason that if you have to apply a correction you have the proper equipment on your dog. Be prepared for politically correct comments you'll receive from other "Sophisticated" dog owners like, "Oh my gosh, your using a CHOKE CHAIN!" or "Don't you know your killing your dog!" Politely remind them that it is a *chain collar* and is only referred to as a *choke chain* when it is used incorrectly.

Just like fishing when you feel the tug on the lead apply a correction snapping the lead and immediately switch directions and if your dog starts to pull on the lead again, apply another correction and switch directions. If your dogs insist on leading the walk, remember emulate a ping-pong ball by changing directions. Your dogs should get the message fairly quickly, if not, promptly end the walk. You may find that you'll repeat this exercise a half dozen times before they get the message.

Once you've gained control over your subordinates the next challenge will be, "What happens when you all encounter the unexpected?" By that I mean another dog, person, or animal. As far as the pack is concerned their den is home and their territory as far as their line of sight and in no uncertain terms is anything or anyone allowed within the territory without permission of the Alphas.

It has been my experience that it is easy to predict the behavior of the dog by examining the behavior of the owner. If the owner is lacking a calm demeanor, then typically their dogs will lack confidence. For example, if a strange dog approaches the owner and he or she starts screaming at it to go away the reaction from their dogs will usually be some type of aggression towards the offender. If the owner is calm, the strange dog will usually exchange pleasantries with the pack and continue on none the worse for wear.

When walking outdoors expect the unexpected. What I mean by this is be on guard and prepared to act calmly if you encounter a potential threat. So many dog owners allow their dogs off lead with the notion that their dog won't start a fight. The fact is that seldom do these dogs start fights; rather the fight comes to them when they encounter a dog that has a nervous owner attached to end of the lead.

Whether you're firmly established as Alpha or a subordinate pack member your dogs will alert you of a threat. It is how you respond to the threat that has a profound impact on your dogs. I see so many owners yell at their dogs to stop barking when all they are doing is their job, alerting the pack of a threat. Imagine from the dog's perspective; they're facing a threat with their owner behind them yelling something incomprehensible. From this stance our dogs think that we're standing behind them barking at the same threat they are and that we are too afraid to step out and confront the threat, as Alphas would do in the wild. This sends a pretty strong message that, "Hey, I'm chicken. You're out in front so you all deal with it".

The best tactic to fend off a threat during a walk and send the Alpha message is to position yourself between the dogs and the threat, tell them "Good boys, good girls!" Put the dogs in a sit position and calmly tell them to stay. This sends the message a) threat acknowledged, "I the Alpha am dealing with it", and b) Alpha says, "It's not a threat to be concerned with." Taking your pack on a walk can be one of the most enjoyable parts of being a dog owner. Just remember to take the lead.

CASE STUDY: THE DOG THAT PULLED TOO HARD

One of the most compelling cases I have dealt with is Libby, a beautiful 5-year-old Boxer female that had been adopted by elderly couple in a nearby town. The local rescue group had referred them to me after receiving a call that Libby had dragged the owner several feet during a recent walk.

The owners had had Libby for about three weeks and couldn't understand why all of sudden she started acting out. Their comment to me was that she had been a perfect angel until only recently when she had started showing aggression towards passersby. The most recent incident had Libby attached via a retractable lead on a walk at the local greenbelt when Libby spotted another dog off in the distance. Libby decided that she didn't much care for this particular dog so she took off full speed barking and snarling. Just like a fish on the hook, the retractable lead provided slack until it reached the end of the spool. Being a good owner, the thought was "... there is no way I am letting go of this contraption and have a dog fight on my hands".

Naturally, upon reaching the end of the line the dog owner went flying much like a water skier starting a run and was promptly dragged ten feet bruising his ribs in the process. Luckily by the time they called me they had a sense of humor over the whole episode. The icebreaker was when I told them. "... Now you know why I don't recommend retractable leads for dogs over 40 lbs".

One of the interesting dynamics in this case was the length of time Libby had been in the household. Rescue dogs that are in foster homes tend to get moved often and regardless of the dog's circumstances there are two important milestones to remember when entering a new household. The first 48 hours are crucial. During this time the dog is in a virtual haze and it's not sure of its coming or going. What I strongly recommend is that the dog be tethered to the owner at all times (umbilical cord technique) unless it is in the kennel. This develops a bond between dog and human that begins the process of establishing the Alpha role.

The next milestone is the two to three week mark. At this point the dog realizes that it is in its permanent den and must sort out the hierarchy of the pack. If there is no Alpha present it will assume this role quickly (or try to). In Libby's case the time had come, she was Alpha, and she would protect her pack members with extreme prejudice, hence the overall aggressive posturing with passersby and rival dogs at the greenbelt. Fortunately neither dog nor human had been badly injured yet as result of Libby's aggression.

As with every evaluation and consultation we began with the sleeping location and in this case Libby was sleeping on the bedroom floor with the bedroom door open. The point was made to the owners that Libby is sleeping where she wants. She is simply choosing to sleep near you so that she can monitor and protect you as the Alpha. Getting Libby kennel trained was fairly easy and she adapted to it within a couple of days with no issues. We also examined the feeding routine for Libby and discovered that she was allowed to eat freely from the dog bowl anytime during the day. Again we pointed out to the owners how this was inappropriate in that it was sending Libby the message that she was high-ranking member of the pack. We reviewed the feeding guidelines with the owners and started Libby on the feeding routine. The next step was to get Libby under control during the walk.

Getting Libby under control for the walk was going to be a bit more challenging then kennel training and the Alpha feeding routine. Libby was very strong and the owners were getting on in years. The fear was that if we had another episode were the dog knocked the owner off its feet that we may have a fracture and with most elderly people this can be a devastating injury. First order of business was to advise the owners to ditch the retractable lead and switch to a 6-foot lead with chain collar for Libby. The key for success would be training the owners on how they would have to control Libby. In cases like this we recommend the owners follow the program guidelines while simultaneously putting their dog through a basic obedience program. The most important things to be gained for any canine obedience-training program are learning how to control and communicate with your dog, while building the dog's confidence.

The decision was made to hold off on taking Libby on any outside walks until the owners had completed the basic obedience-training program. Most effective basic obedience programs take about 12 weeks to complete with a half dozen or so detailed training sessions. Later on in the book we outline a basic obedience-training program. Having completed the training program the owners felt confident that they knew what to do in the event that Libby encountered the unexpected during the walk.

So now it was time to test the owner's new abilities and see how Libby would respond. We scheduled a session at the greenbelt during a time when there would be a lot of traffic coming and going from the park. Prior to heading to the greenbelt we had decided that if Libby encountered another person or dog being walked and if she showed any anxiety that she would be placed in a sitting stay position at the owner's side. As we began to walk on the greenbelt path we noticed another dog owner approaching some 50 yards away, almost instantly Libby came to attention and began to develop signs of heightened anticipation. As we had agreed when the pair got to about the 10 yard mark the owner placed Libby in sitting stay position on the left side of the owner. When the pair got to the 5-yard mark Libby attempted to get out of the sitting stay position. The owner responded quickly with a lead correction and when Libby made eye contact the owner gave her immediate positive praise returning her to the sitting stay position. The pair quietly passed by without incident.

This was a huge milestone in Libby's development. Three months earlier she would have made an all out assault to get to the pair walking by. Now she simply responded and obeyed the command of the Alpha. From this point forward Libby was able to enjoy walks with her master with no incidents of aggressive behavior towards dogs or passersby.

CASE STUDY: THE DOOR DASHER

One canine trait that has always interested me is a characteristic termed "Prey Drive". It manifests itself in a couple of different ways with one common denominator; pure focus. The dogs that are driven by prey (or chase of the hunt) are relentless in their pursuit. A great example of this is my wife's favorite dog (don't tell the others it has always been her secret) is 6-year-old miniature dachshund named Lilly. Lilly will literally chase a tossed ball or object until she would drop dead from exhaustion. Anytime we have a visitor to the house Lilly will greet the visitor by tossing a ball or object towards the newcomer insisting that the game (or chase of the hunt) begin. This type of behavior in the overall scheme of things is not dangerous or harmful and in my mind rather amusing. One of the manifestations of prey drive that is not so amusing is what we call door dashing.

We recently received a call from a local rescue group about a beautiful 1-year-old female Boxer named Izzy. Izzy had recently been adopted and had the propensity to dash out the front door when the opportunity arose and would chase passing cars on a local road. To make matters worse when the owner would try to catch her she would keep running from them. Izzy, being very athletic, could probably win a gold medal at the canine Olympics in any type of running event she was un-catch-able. Typically after a few hours the owners would get a call from the neighbors saying that they had Izzy and would they come retrieve her. The dashing had occurred a couple of times, but the event that sparked the call to us was that the neighbor had witnessed Izzy get hit by car sending her rolling into the median. Fortunately Izzy only had a few scrapes and bruises being none the worse for wear.

For this type of behavior my curiosity has always been, "what does the dog think is outside just around the corner out of sight" and "what compels the dog to go after it". In Izzy's case it was those big metal boxes with round legs that move at about 35 mph. After spending a few minutes with Izzy it was clear to both owner and I that Izzy had assumed the Alpha role and was intent upon leading the hunt after those big metal boxes. Beyond the normal establishing Alpha there were a couple of techniques we were going to have to focus on right away, threshold respect, come command, and walking on lead.

Not only was Izzy athletic but also very intelligent. We had started working with her initially on threshold respect the back patio door with good success, but she was still dashing out the front door on occasion. We progressed to a 30-foot lead and would entice her out the front door to provide a snap back correction with the lead (something like a bungee cord). This seemed to work, but a month or so later she again door dashed. This now called for stronger measures to get the situation corrected. Coupled with this activity we were also working with the come command and walking on lead.

Izzy had been progressing very nicely through the basic obedience program having mastered the basics and was doing well with the come command on a 30 foot lead. Izzy had greatly improved during her walks and was no longer pulling on the lead. The owners had done a good job establishing Alpha in the household. We had started to work on the come command off lead and this is where Izzy struggled. Clearly she had gotten "leash smart", a term trainer's use when the dogs knows it can be corrected via lead. Being off lead meant that Izzy at worst would receive a verbal correction, not something you want to do when training a dog to respond to the come command. The come command is the most important of all commands. It means drop what your doing and "B line" to me. Note: this is a very important command to perfect when a car is bearing down on your dog and you need to get it to move out of the way. Now the question became how to get Izzy to respect thresholds and respond to the come command. This is an excellent example were an electronic collar can be very effective.

When training with an electronic collar the goal is to make the dog respect the issue (thresholds, Snakes, windows, etc.) and think your voice is magic because you can send corrections from a distance. It is very important that the electronic collar get deployed properly. Improper use can destroy a dog's confidence and produce a very fearful or timid dog. If you're not sure how to use one seek the help of a professional trainer it is well worth the expense.

We first focused on the come command while using the electronic collar to make sure that Izzy would respond positively. After she had mastered the come command from a distance without the collar we moved to instilling threshold respect by not passing the entry areas to the garage or front door. It took a few weeks but Izzy no longer tries to bolt out open doors and responds much better on her walks.

CHAPTER 5
SPEAKING A DOG'S LANGUAGE
SILENT COMMUNICATIONS

As humans we communicate ninety five percent verbally and five percent using body language. With our dogs it is exactly the opposite, ninety five percent body language and only five percent verbal. During a consultation and typically within the first thirty minutes, I can point out at least half dozen or so silent signals the dog has sent the owner. Subtle things like placing their paw on the foot, leaning against the owner, or body positioning. All very strong silent signals sent with expectation of a response from the owner either affirming or rejecting the message. Most owners are completely unaware of these subtle interactions and their lack of appropriate response only affirms the dog's position in the pack.

We have all heard of a "Yes dear" conversation. It's that conversation with our significant other who really isn't listening to us, but is simply responding "Yes dear" to every thing we say. Imagine our dogs, sending us a message via body language translated something like, "Hey, why don't you get up and let me the "Alpha" out the patio door, I'm waiting" or " … come on pet me the "Alpha", can't you see that I have my paw on your foot, I am waiting." As is human nature we comply by letting them out or petting them and all the while we're saying, "Yes, Dear …, Yes, dear …., Yes, dear."

Now what to look for is the golden question? In general any time our dogs physically interact with us whether it is a nip, a bite, or a light touch, it is a form of communication. Whenever our dogs interact with us in anyway that intersects with our physical space, it is a form of communication. One of the most recognizable communiqués is when ours dogs jump on us, note this is only one form, there are multitudes of others. It is how we react and respond to the communication that sends the message to our dogs that we are the Alpha in charge. Communicating with our dogs non-verbally is key. We have to make sure that when we see the physical message that we respond to it in kind, physically.

Jumping is the simplest silent communiqué to recognize and the easiest to respond to. Jumping pure and simple is a sign of dominance. No matter the stature of the dog whether it is a Miniature Dachshund or Great Dane when they jump they are trying to get their eye level to our eye level. The instant they think they have achieved eye level and their paws make contact they are saying unequivocally, "Welcome to my domain, I am the Alpha and you better take notice ..." As humans when we backup, turn to the side, or otherwise not challenge the dog we have just affirmed their assertion, without speaking one word. Now if you're like me, we don't want our dogs ruling the household so there is one effective way to counter this message and it is a simple one. When they jump, take away their space. Do this by stepping into the jump and raising a knee, take note not to use your hands to push the dog away. Do not make verbal or eye contact when doing so. This sends the immediate message back that, "This is not your domain, you have no standing with me and there will be no negotiation."

Now that we've gotten past the jumping, expect the next set of communiqués to become more subtle. The dog's personality will dictate the delivery but their message will be consistent, "No, your mistaken. This IS my domain, I am the Alpha and you better take notice ..." Depending on the age of the dog this interaction may go on for an extended period of time. The key is to remember that when the dog intersects with your physical space your reaction is always a simple one. In turn take away their space. An example of a very subtle but strong communiqué is when we have a dog sit close to us and place their paw on our foot. Of all the hundreds of places the dog could have placed its paw it chose to put it on top of the foot. Believe me it is not by accident, but by design. To simple ignore the paw on the foot would be saying to our dog that, "Hey, you know you might be in charge."

To send the appropriate response without saying a word, simply tap on the top of their paw with the bottom of your shoe. This sends a nice crisp message that, "Excuse me, let me remind you again this is not your domain, you have no standing with me, and there will be no negotiation." It is very important that you remain calm, confident, and consistent when you're communicating with your dog. The tap on foot should be a matter of fact, a period, not an exclamation point.

A classic case of silent communication is what I characterize as the *"leaning dog."* We've all seen this. We can be sitting in our family rooms watching TV, standing talking to a family member or simply relaxing in our easy chair reading the paper and our dog will come up very quietly and lean against us. For most people the force of habit is to lean over and pet the dog. You probably can already see where I am going with this. The dog approached and without a sound intersected with my physical space clearly stated, "Pet me, as a high-ranking member of the pack I deserve affection on my terms". The appropriate response again is a simple one; take away their space. Bump them off and communicate with them by stating their name, "Hey buddy how's it going, what are you doing?" This acknowledges to your dog that you know that they are there and that you know that he or she is trying to communicate with you. At this juncture your dog will either lean into you at which point you will bump them off again or choose to sit down with space separating the two of you. The moment your dog sits down with space separating the two of you, you just won the argument, "I am Alpha and I will determine the way in which I give out affection".

In all physical interactions the dog is accessing your leadership and if found lacking they will attempt to assert their dominance. It is instinctive and insures preservation of the pack. Often owners of rescue dogs will choose to have their dogs go through a basic obedience program. There are many good reasons to do so, primarily building the dogs confidence, providing them a "job", and accelerating the Alpha principle. During basic obedience the subtle silent communiqués are never more evident then when learning and performing Heel. During a Heel session you can be guaranteed that if dog has an Alpha complex it will demonstrate a least a half dozen signs of dominance.

When we are called out on a consultation, one of the tools we use is Heel. Even if the dog is unfamiliar with it, we take the time to initiate the walk with me, stop with me routine (covered later in basic obedience). This basically dictates that dog walks on our left side and when we stop it assumes a sitting position directly opposite our left hip. It is amazing to see how many other spots then directly off the left hip the dog may sit with each adaptation underscoring their Alpha complex. Once we get the dog performing properly we hand the leash to the owner and take note of the number of silent communiqués during a Heel. We review each subtle communication and outline the appropriate response. After a few minutes the owners realize how much canine conversation has occurred and the most effective ways to communicate Alpha during a Heel.

CASE STUDY: JUMPIN GEHOSAFAT

One of the most common complaints about bad canine behavior is dogs that jump on their owners or house guests. This is very annoying behavior especially with bigger dogs that can cause personal injury as is the case with small children or the elderly that get knocked to the ground. When a dog jumps it is because they seek our undivided attention. Remember when a dog jumps on us and intersects with our physical space they are sending us a message. "… Hey you, I want attention on my terms and as high ranking member of the pack I deserve it." How we respond is very important in sending our dog the correct message, "… no, as Alpha I dictate under what terms I give out affection."

A very intriguing case was one that involved a foster mom for a local Boxer rescue group. In this particular case the foster mom had 4 Boxers and a beagle in her care with all but one of the Boxer's being deaf. Anytime the foster mom would return home from a trip the dogs would proceed to jump, I mean all the dogs. Imagine the scene, 5 dogs jumping up and down as though they were on pogo sticks. More intriguing was the only Boxer that was coming into contact with guests or the owner while jumping was the Boxer that had its full hearing. When I inquired about the behavior the foster mom noted that this was a ritual she encountered every day when she returned from work.

As I made my observations it became very clear that the Boxer with full hearing had assumed the Alpha role within the pack. This would be a very natural occurrence in the wild. Naturally the stronger and in this case the dog without any impairments would assume the Alpha role by default. Even more interesting was the ritual the owner went through each time she returned home. Immediately upon entering the Den she would engage each dog in effort to calm the chaos. With each individual interaction I noted that each dog wagged its tail and would lean back into the owner while looking to be petted. Without knowing it the foster mom was mimicking a type of greeting ritual that occurs with wild wolf packs.

Whenever we leave our pets at home for any length of time our dogs instinctively assume that we have gone out on a scouting mission. When Alphas depart on a scouting mission there are three likely outcomes; one the Alpha is killed and never returns, two the returning Alpha is injured and is unable to maintain its role, or three the Alpha returns intact and in charge. The injured Alpha returning to the den will immediately upon entry socialize with each pack member. The healthy Alpha returning to the den will simply ignore other pack members as though they are background noise until the Alpha decides it is time to heap out affection on the pack member of its choosing. So ten years ago before I became "dog savvy" I would return from work and upon entering the house would say, "Hey buddy, how are you doing today?" Remember dogs don't understand language but recognize words. So you can imagine what was going through my dog's mind. Buddy would come up wagging his tail and lean his back into me as if to say, "Okay, what happened out there that you're trying to tell me that is keeping you from being Alpha." All the while by leaning into me he was assuming a dominant posture without any physical response from me was only reinforcing the message that I was no longer able to be Alpha.

I related this story to the foster mom and underscored two key principles that separate dogs from humans. First dogs live in the here and now and do not have the concept of time so anytime we are out of eyeshot, earshot, or smell range and when we return our dogs don't know if we have been gone five minutes or five hours. Secondly, dogs don't understand language but recognize words and at most can associate ten to twenty human words with their name, commands, food, or stop activity. Understanding this, it was crucial to engage in the greeting ritual the same way upon returning home and that is to completely ignore the dogs until they have been calm a full five minutes, meaning no eye, verbal, or physical contact during this time. Keeping steadfast to this routine would only build confidence in the dogs that nothing had happened that would keep her from performing her Alpha duties and responsibilities. I am glad to report that after a few weeks of following the guidelines, returning to the house became a much more orderly exercise.

JOHN KALEVI SIEVILA

CASE STUDY: IN YOUR FACE

So far we've discussed mostly subtle physical posturing dogs do to communicate with us. One form of communication that is not subtle is when a dog bites or nips us. In the wild when dogs correct one another they will bite or nip, unfortunately when dogs attempt to correct humans by biting or nipping they will break the skin and cause puncture wounds. Obviously this is unacceptable behavior for domesticated dogs. But note that when a dog nips us they're not doing it out of aggression but out of dominance. It is their way of correcting us for bad behavior. This leads us to our next case study which involves a three-year-old boy being bit by a Boxer.

It is rare but does happen on occasion where a dog will bit a young human. In these cases the dog is not biting because it perceives the youngster as a threat, but more so is biting to perform a correction. Every once in while you'll get a call where you just have to ask yourself, "Did I hear what I just thought I heard." The call started off by the mother of the three year old telling me that the dog had bit her son's face. I asked the mother if there was anything that had precipitated the event and she said that the two had been together in the family room where her son had been blowing air into the dog's face. Now in dog language this would be considered an insult. But on the face of it a three year old blowing air into the face of a dog should not cause the dog bite. I went on to ask the mother were there any other indications that the dog might bite. She did say, "Come to think of it Brandon had urinated on Bruno the day before."

At this point I had to say, "Timeout, I'm confused here is Brandon your son and Bruno your dog or visa versa?" The mother replied, "Bruno is our dog and Brandon is our three year old". I thanked the mother for the clarification and made the point that in this case what Brandon had done was simply the worst insult a dog could receive. In fact, Bruno had been doing his job in correcting a younger member of the pack and that the issue was more the supervision of the three year old rather than the dog. I spent the next several minutes reviewing our program guidelines and how to establish Alpha within the household. I also stressed with the mother how important it was to monitor the interactions between Brandon and Bruno. Not only was this a good idea but that she was ultimately responsible for Brandon's and Bruno's well being.

THE DOG REDEEMERS

Though this is not a typical call the rescue groups receive it is symptomatic of an underlying problem. Typically when people bring puppies into their homes they fail to properly perform puppy imprinting. Often times when people fail to properly raise a puppy it will wind up in rescue. People make the mistake of thinking that it is okay for a puppy to bite our hands or excessively lick our hands when we're playing with them. What we're doing from an early age is teaching the dog that is acceptable to put their open mouth on a human. So that when they get older if they decide to correct the human it is acceptable to do so with their mouth, by biting or nipping us. In our methodology it is never acceptable for a dog to put their open mouth on our hands or feet. For older dogs, to correct this behavior we will encourage them to put their open mouth on our hands or excessively lick (more then 2 licks in succession) and when they do we provide a severe correction using a leash and chain collar. For puppies, as part of puppy imprinting, we simply perform physical manipulation using our hands on their mouths and paws so that they get used to human contact. In this case since Bruno had been a puppy he had been allowed to roughhouse using his open mouth. In this particular case we performed an in-home consultation and came to the conclusion that the environment was not suitable for Bruno. In reality the mother had difficulty maintaining a stable household with several young children and said it would be very difficult if not impossible to rehabilitate Bruno.

This is a good example of how every home environment may not be suitable for dogs and in these cases dogs should be turned into rescue for adoption.

CHAPTER 6
HOUSEBREAKING
ACCIDENTS ON PURPOSE

One of the most frequent calls that rescue groups receive for an owner turn-in is due to the canine urinating or defecating in the house. For puppies or adolescent dogs the most common excuse is that he or she doesn't quite get the concept of going "potty" outside. In reality the dog owners usually don't have a clue on proper housebreaking training. For older dogs that at one point were housebroken (or so the owners claim) and started urinating or defecating in the house was another very common reason for owner turn ins to rescue groups. No dog should ever be turned into a rescue group for urinating or defecating in the house. Even in cases where there are health concerns a vet visit can usually correct the problem. Here are the rules on housebreaking; puppies or adolescent dogs don't have accidents, it's an accident on the owner's part for lack of attention and supervision. Older dogs don't have accidents in their dens (notice I state *"their")*, they mark in them.

Housebreaking a dog can be very traumatic for both owner and dog. A high percentage of dog abuse starts when emotional owners get out of control when attempting to housebreak (traumatic housebreaking) a dog. This can cause the most damage for young adolescent dogs. At two to four months of age dogs form the personalities that will take them through their adulthood. It is critical that during this time period we ensure there are no traumatic experiences that could effect the overall personality development of the dog. A dog eating its own feces (Feces eating disorder) is one behavior stemming from traumatic housebreaking.

To understand what causes this behavior we need to realize how dogs process events. For example if our dog starts to "potty" on our living room carpet we process the event as follows: Dog going "potty" + dog on brand new living room carpet = "NOOOO! (Vein popping)" + throw dog outside. Now we processed several points during this event with the trigger point being the dog going potty which caused an emotional outburst from us. Our dogs simply process the trigger point and then shut down the instant we invoke an emotional outburst. They see it as not going "potty" on the living room carpet = bad, but going "potty" in front of you period = bad. Since "potty" in front of you is bad, next chance they get they will try to hide the activity from you.

Now compound this with the time element. You have a history of outbursts; imagine you've returned home from day at work to find feces on the floor. Boom you go ballistic! Remember your dogs concept of time is different then ours, if you were gone for fifteen minutes or more they don't know if its been five minutes or five hours. So here is how we process the event: Sight feces on floor + pickup feces while yelling at the dog = throw the dog outside. Again our dog processes up to the trigger point and shuts down, in this case you picking up the feces. From our dog's perspective you entered the den started yelling and then proceeded to pick up the feces. They don't equate that going "potty" is bad, just that feces are bad. Remember too much time has passed and by now they don't even remember going "potty". Repeating this same behavior will eventually cause the dog to eat its own feces to hide the offence. Doing this with a young dog between the ages of two to four months increases the feces eating disorder twenty fold.

Not to worry, housebreaking isn't rocket surgery (combination of rocket science and brain surgery), as colleague of mine would interject. The technique to correct the behavior is straight forward, but the key is attitude. When it comes to housebreaking the first topic I cover is that we all have busy schedules and we need to set the expectation within ourselves that this is going to take time, effort, and patience. After all we don't get rid of our children if it takes a couple of months to potty train them. Setting the expectation, remaining calm, confident, and consistent is the foundation for successfully housebreaking a dog. Whether the offending dog is a puppy, adolescent, or mature dog the next key ingredient is that they do not go unsupervised until they are completely housebroken. Yes, completely means no mistakes for at least 2 weeks.

This has to go in lock step with establishing yourself as the Alpha in charge of the den and pack. Not doing so will cause your dogs to potentially have a relapse if the dynamics of the pack or den change.

To adequately supervise your dogs there is a simple but hard fast rule; when they are out of their kennels (or crates) in the house (den) they are on lead and collar and attached to your belt loop (referred to as umbilical cord technique). This is very important point, your dogs are not connected to you so that you can apply a correction in the event they start to urinate or defecate. They are connected so that you'll pay attention and supervise their activity while in the house. When (not if) they do start to defecate or urinate in the house interrupt the activity remaining calm, take them outside and when they finish their business a huge fourth of July type of praise party in their honor. Interrupting the activity means to calmly distract the dog, not to yell (common mistake amongst dog owners). First, the dogs begin to understand that every time they start to urinate or defecate in the house they get interrupted and dogs do not like to be interrupted. Secondly, when taken outside to finish they get all sorts of love and attention that dogs desperately crave. Results are a win-win and a housebroken dog.

Unfortunately dogs cannot be programmed and there can be what appears to be episodes of backsliding specifically with males in particular. Over the years there is one behavior that I've observed time and time again; a small percentage of males will continue to have the urge to mark the perimeter of the den either just outside or inside the entry way. Usually what precipitates this event is if there is any type of activity that involves either strangers or new dogs coming into the household. The upheaval (in their minds) causes the dogs to want to mark their scent at the entry ways so the visitors will take note that this is their pack's den. With this type of behavior a different tactic is needed to correct the marking episodes. In this case a correction is called for, either verbal "NO" or if on lead a snap correction both followed by instant positive praise "Good Boy!" You usually can pick these dogs out from a crowd because they will be the ones that tend to mark a lot when they are out in neutral ground (e.g. public areas, dog parks, etc.). So be prepared if you find yourself in these circumstances to apply the proper correction.

CASE STUDY: THE ACCIDENTAL CANINE

Barnaby was a 5-month-old Cocker Spaniel that had been an owner turn-in to a local rescue group for urinating in the house. Barnaby had been staying at a local pet resort where I was asked to go out and do an evaluation. Staff warned me that Barnaby had submissive urination to the extreme. Usually I take these things with a grain of salt but in this case I could not believe my eyes when they brought Barnaby out to me. As handler and dog approached, from some 25 feet away, I could see Barnaby submissive urinating in a spurting stream that extended about 2 to 3 feet ahead. I was absolutely flabbergasted. My first thought was there was something about me that was intimidating, so I asked the handler, "Does he do this with everyone?". The handler somewhat bewildered responded, "Not only everyone but every known creature it seems". During the evaluation it became evident that Barnaby was truly a gentle dog with no signs of aggression and only lacked confidence.

Next my range of emotions quickly shifted from amazement to worry. How would Barnaby ever get adopted if he continued submissive urination in this way? Not fully knowing Barnaby's background or to what level of abuse he had received it was going to be difficult to come up with a regiment that would cure the problem. My thoughts raced back to one of the first dogs that I had ever worked with. She was a beautiful longhaired dachshund named Duchess. Duchess had been rescued from a puppy mill where she had been used for breeding. Duchess spent 24/7 in the kennel, much like a hen in an egg farm. Duchess would urinate anywhere and everywhere, in her kennel or in the house, it didn't matter. What finally cured her was that the instant she urinated in her kennel we would take her out and give her a bath. Same thing if she showed submissive urination out of the kennel. Each time staying calm and not saying a word until the bath was over. What I soon discovered is that most dogs don't enjoy baths, they tolerate them. Duchess soon discovered that urinating in the wrong place meant a bath and in the right place outside meant positive praise.

So the plan for Barnaby was to come spend a couple of weeks at my house in a sort of mini boot camp to see if we could get the behavior corrected using the bath method. At that time I had another cocker in the house named Lucy (who you'll learn about in another case study) who would become Barnaby's mentor.

We established a daily ritual where each morning Lucy and I would greet Barnaby and release him from his kennel. I would make sure that he was not allowed out the kennel door (threshold respect) until he got the magic words from me "OK!" This was his first signal of the day that I was the Alpha in charge. Barnaby would promptly exit the kennel to submissive urinate all over my laundry room floor. Without a word I picked up Barnaby and proceeded to give him a bath. Upon completing the bath it was time to head back to the laundry room to feed Barnaby.

Back in the laundry room we followed the feeding ritual to the letter, not allowing Barnaby to eat until the dog bowl could be left on the floor and the magic words invoked "OK" allowing him to eat, again sending a clear message that I am the Alpha in charge. Next step was the umbilical cord technique. Barnaby was attached to my belt loop via lead and collar with Lucy in close quarters and we proceeded to explore the surroundings, all the while Lucy nor I showing any signs of anxiety whenever Barnaby would become a little nervous. We continued this routine for a week, with every episode of submissive urination accompanied by a bath. By the end of the first week the submissive urination had dramatically subsided.

The following week we built on the successes of the first week and taught Barnaby heel and down commands. Three training sessions daily lasting about 10 minutes with tons of positive praise worked very well for Barnaby. By the end of the second week nearly all signs of submissive urination had ceased. Barnaby returned back to the pet resort and I worked with the staff to continue the training regiment. I am glad to report after four more weeks of work Barnaby was adopted by a local family. Mission accomplished.

CASE STUDY: PISSING CONTEST

Today we live in what I term a "Fast Food" society where too often people want an instant fix for everything including their canine problems. In the past few years' dogs have been equated rights and elevated status to that of surrogate children. It might just be me, but as child I remember growing up and dogs where just dogs. We didn't have the fear that a loose dog running about was going to cause us grave concern unless it was foaming at the mouth. We would simply corral the dog; play with it for a while until it either left to return home or the wayward owner showed up. But in today's world the perception of dogs has changed in some ways for the better and some for the worse. One thing has remained the same for millennia and that is dogs are very complex creatures, each unique, and each having its own quirky personality. In working with dog owners I consistently remind them that dogs are not machines to be programmed, so expect the unexpected.

One can usually count on the unexpected when a new dog is introduced into a household that has an established set of dogs. I have had several cases were new dogs have been introduced and low and behold new instances of urinating in the house have occurred, even though all the dogs have been housebroken or so the owner would attest to. I consistently inform owners that any dog past the age of sixteen weeks can be housebroken within two weeks provided it is healthy. It boils down to two facets either the dog was not housebroken properly or it is simply choosing to urinate in the house. If the dog chooses to urinate in the house it is doing so either as a test or because it already believes it is Alpha and is entitled to mark its den in anyway it desires.

This particular case study deals with the introduction of a new dog named Sadie into a household with two established Boxers named Kelsey and Morgan. Both Kelsey and Morgan had been through basic obedience training and had been housebroken as puppies. Sadie was an older Boxer that had come through rescue with an unknown history (very common). At first the owner would discover urination spots in different areas of the house and it was unclear who the perpetrator was. Clearly in the owners mind it must be Sadie, because there had been no problems before her arrival. Obviously Sadie had not been properly housebroken or so was the conclusion the owner came too. Sound logic but wrong conclusion, the key piece of evidence here was that no-one had seen any of the dogs urinate in house. A definite clue that all the dogs had gone through some type of housebreaking in the past, most likely old school where you caught the dog in the act yelled "No!" and tossed it outside. Note that the dogs where hiding the act so as not to be corrected. The main concern for the owner was how to correct the problem.

The prescription had to have a two prong approach; establishing Alpha in the household and absolute monitoring and supervision while in the house. Anytime a new dog is introduced into a household it is an unsettling time for the pack. For pack members it is almost complete chaos for the first two to three weeks. Established pack members look to see if the new dog has potential to become Alpha of the pack and looks to the owners to see that challenges from the new rival are dealt with. In this case the owners had never established Alpha in the household, so truth be told all three dogs were urinating in the house in sort of a "Pissing contest" to see whose scent would mark the interior of the den. I advised the owners it was back to square one on housebreaking and walked them through the process in addition to following the program guidelines of establishing the Alpha within the household. It took considerable time and effort from the owner but after a few weeks there is no more urination in the house.

CHAPTER 7
BARKING
THE ART OF DIPLOMACY

Dogs basically bark for three reasons; to signal their location to the pack, alert the pack of a threat, or simply to vocalize an emotion. Dogs can typically recognize the type of bark of another dog by the successive frequency of barks and type of bark. A good example of a dog signaling its location to the pack is the common howl we hear from beagles. A dog warning of a threat sounds off a series of successive sharp barks to alert the intruder that it has been detected and also send a message to the other pack members that there is danger a foot. Vocalization of emotions for dogs can come in many forms from a growl, whimper, cry or yodel. This is the dog's form of verbal communication. Remember that dogs don't understand language but recognize words, so it is the combination of body posturing and vocalization that makes up the dog's language. One thing to keep in mind is that dogs at best have a vocabulary of ten to twenty words that they associate with their name, commands, or stop activity. So for us to effectively communicate with our dogs we have to combine language with body posturing to send the correct message. The challenge becomes how to control our dog's barking.

It is interesting how certain breeds have distinguishing barks none more distinctive then that of the hound family. When hounds howl it seems that the sound can carry for miles, so more often then not one of the first calls I receive from a foster with a new hound is a howling problem. The reoccurring theme is that the dog is out in the backyard and won't stop howling. I explain that during the first 48 hours the dog is in your care it believes it is in a migration and doesn't know if its coming or going. The dog believes that at that moment it has been separated from its pack it is duty bound to signal its location to the pack by howling. I warn the foster that this behavior is likely to continue for a few days but will subside once the dog has accepted its new location as its den and new pack. In order to keep the howling at a minimum the best method is distraction and to refocus the dog's attention on other matters such a play or exercise. In severe cases I have recommended that the dog be placed on an umbilical cord (leash connected to belt loop of adult) for a couple of days to help alleviate the dog's anxiety. The good news is that this type of barking can be easily controlled.

To some people there is nothing more annoying than a dog barking constantly. For most dog owners only when barking becomes repetitive and excessive does it becomes annoying. For the most part we've learned to ignore the occasional bark and only take notice when the bark takes on a completely different tone. As dog owners we can often recognize the difference between a "normal" bark and an alarm. The important factor here is how we respond to the sound of the alarm bark. It is each pack member's responsibility to alert the pack of a perceived threat. It is the Alpha's responsibility to access the threat and take appropriate measures to ensure safety of the pack. When our dogs' alert us of a perceived threat there is only one correct way to respond and that is to position yourself between the dog and the perceived threat, place an open palm to the face of the canine cupping the muzzle gently and state firmly "enough". This signals the dog that you have accessed the threat and there is no need for concern. To often owners will stand behind the dog while it is barking and say, "No bark", "Stop barking", or "Quiet"! Remember dogs don't understand language but recognize words and body posture, so from their point of view you're barking at the same thing they are but you're too afraid to go out and confront the threat.

There are certain types of barks that we don't want to stifle but nurture. When we engage our dogs' vocalizing we accomplish two things in particular; we forge a stronger emotional bond with our dogs and we build the dog's self confidence. I am often amused by the different sound dogs generate when they are vocalizing their emotions. My daughter has a 2 year old long haired dapple dachshund named "Gunner", who yodels just like a Wookiee from Star Wars with every greeting and at feeding time. At first I didn't know what to make of the yodel and Gunner being a rescue dog had been abused and lacked confidence. In the beginning I encouraged my daughter to respond in kind when the yodeling started by saying, "Gunner your a good boy!" In time I noticed that Gunner's confidence increased twenty fold and that he and my daughter forged a bond that makes them nearly inseparable making him a great companion and excellent family dog.

CASE STUDY: EXCESSIVE BARKING

Alas not all problems can be corrected and this case study centers around my wife's favorite a six year old nine pound miniature dachshund named "Lilly", who is a chronic barker. One characteristic dog's have that have been passed on through generations is prey drive. Prey drive can manifest itself in a couple of different ways in domestic canines; such as a dog that loves to relentlessly chase objects (balls, Frisbees, cars, etc.) or when a dog shows pure focus on something (birds, cats, etc.). Most dogs will have different levels of prey drive; in Lilly's case she has extremely strong prey drive. She will chase a ball until she will literally pass out from exhaustion. So why do strong prey drive dogs tend to bark a lot? Simply put they want the object of their attention to start to flee so that they can chase them down in a hunt. Because they have such a strong prey drive the smallest noise will set them to barking so as to flush the instigator out into a chase.

Although this characteristic represents only a small percentage of the dog population (probably less than 5 %) no amount of training or applied Alpha will correct the excessive barking. To make matters worse for multiple dog households when one starts the barking the rest will chime in starting a chorus of barking. This is probably okay if your closest neighbor lives some distance away, but for most of us this type of noise is frowned upon by your neighbors and HOA(s) (Home Owners Associations). In some cases dog owners have been issued citations or fines from their HOA for dogs that bark excessively (longer than 5 minutes).

Fortunately with today's technology there are tools we can use to control the barking. In my work with rescue groups I am often asked what to do about barking and always make the point that bark collars should only be used as a last resort and that as dog owners we should all set our expectations that canines will bark. In this case however there are no options left other than the use of a bark collar to control Lilly's excessive barking. The question becomes what is the most effective bark collar to use? There are several varieties out on the market from ones that simply make sound to inhibit barking, ones that spray citronella (smell bad to dogs), to ones that apply a static stimulus to prevent barking. Typically when I engage in this conversation I try to put a dog's perspective on the best type of bark collar to control the barking.

Let's examine the bark collars that generate a sound when the dog barks. From the prey dog's perspective it begins to bark in order to flush out an object to begin the chase and what the dog hears is that the collar is aiding in making noise. The dog's thought is "… thank you very much, let's see if we can really scare the snot out of this thing to get it to run." So it has been my experience that for strong prey drive dogs bark collars that generate sound don't control barking.

Bark collars that spray citronella to stop barking are just nasty. From the dog's perspective they have initiated a bark to flush prey and now they are getting a nasty smelling spray to stop. The dog's thought is "… holy cow! This thing has glands that can spray like a skunk." Now we've just introduced a method for making the dog more timid and shake its confidence. Dominant dogs will, in spite of the nasty smell, simply ignore it and continue to hunt the prey. In either case I don't recommend this type of collar for strong prey drive canines.

There are several types of electronic static bark collars. Static bark collars that immediately provide static stimulus to a dog when it barks is a bad idea. We do not want to stop all barking; to stop the dogs urge to bark or otherwise vocalize will result in a timid dog lacking self confidence. The best type of static stimulus bark collars are the ones that will generate a warning sound prior to sending the static stimulus and automatically shut off if the dog barks for more than 30 seconds or so. The bonus with this type of collar is that the dog knows when it is on and that barking is not allowed. Using this method allows us to remove the bark collar and let the dog vocalize to its heart's content on occasion. So for Lilly we have her on bark collar in the evenings when we take her into our backyard to control the barking. This technique has worked wonders and made our neighbors much happier.

CASE STUDY: THE INVISIBLE PERPETRATOR

This case study is about two rotund geriatric beagles named Zena and Buster. The owners are DINKS (Double Income No Kids) who have focused a tremendous amount of their love and affection over the past nine years on the raising of their beloved Zena and Buster. To put it simply, they were spoiled. Over the years the couple had been quite content with the living arrangement and happy to dote and spoil the "kids". Not concerned in the least with what other people might think, any bad behavior was tolerated or ignored. At least that was until they moved into new home situated in a golf course community.

All seemed well for the first four or five months until the owners started receiving fines from their HOA (Home Owners Association) for excessive barking. The owners were hard pressed to determine the cause for the barking. Neither dog had barked at the old home and all had been relatively quiet for the first few months in the new home. The owners thought that if they could determine the cause of the barking they would be able to eliminate it. Each time either dog started to bark the owners would head out to the backyard to find the root cause. At first they thought that perhaps golfers standing at a nearby adjoining tee box maybe the problem. But after a few episodes of barking and investigating to find no-one in sight the owners abandoned this as a possibility. The owners were determined and believed that if they could find the cause they could communicate to the dogs that there was nothing to bark about.

It wasn't too long after their third fine that the owners contacted me with an odd request. They wanted me to setup sort of duck blind in the backyard and conduct a stake out for a few hours to determine what the dogs were barking at. When they had told me of their plans I could barely contain my amusement. Out of curiosity I asked them, "What do you intend to do with the information once we determine the perpetrator?" They informed me that they intended to take this information so that when the dogs started barking they would go outside and tell the dogs that it was good, not bad, so stop barking. You can imagine my surprise so I had to think of a logical question that would make them contemplate the best course of action, so I asked the question, "What if we can't see what they are barking at?"

"What do you mean, *what if we can't see what they are barking at?*", the owners replied. I impressed upon the owners that they had Beagles and that at heart both Zena and Buster were hounds. Being hounds they think with their noses, not necessarily with their line of sight. I asked the owners, "Have you ever seen a fox hunt?" "Well, yes", said both owners. "Did you ever notice the dogs barking at the start of the hunt?", I replied. "Yes, most definitely", stated the owners. Now following my lead I asked, "Have the dogs seen the fox yet?" There were a few seconds of silence while the owner contemplated my question, followed by "Ah, yes". The point being that dogs don't necessarily have to see the object which they are barking at, but rather can pick up the scent from some distance. The owners asked, "But what caused them to start barking all of sudden?"

Living in the Southwest it was probably pretty easy to guess what had happened. I asked the question, "Have you seen or have there been any reports of coyotes?" The owners mentioned that they had received a notice from their HOA that coyotes had been spotted on the golf course. They added that on two occasions they had seen them in person, coyotes running through the fairway. I advised them that more then likely a coyote had come up close to the wrought iron fence and caused an incident with the dogs. Now anytime a coyote was passing by upwind and the dogs caught the scent it was causing them to bark to give the coyote warning. It was clear that owners grasped what I had said and simply asked, "What can we do about this?"

I told them the first concern is the safety of the dogs and that they should not be allowed in the backyard when they were away from home. I told them that their fence could have been easily scaled by a coyote but the two things they had going for them was the size of their dogs and that there were two of them. Diplomatically I told them that as overweight as their dogs were a coyote would have had a hard time carrying the body over the fence. You can imagine the look on their faces once I had told them. I knew then that their dogs would never be let out in the backyard while they were away. "How do we curb the barking?", the owners continued.

I explained that to get this quickly under control and to appease the HOA that we needed to consider electronic bark collars. I could tell by the expressions on their faces that they really didn't want to hurt their dogs because of barking. Having seen this expression many times I countered before they could ask the question, "Electronic bark collars provide a stimulus, not a shock." I told them that I would bring out a collar and demonstrate a stimulus on myself and then on them. If they still had objections afterward then we would explore other alternatives. I have performed this acceptance test many times and have yet to have the concept rejected by the owners. The owners having met the test agreed that we should move forward using the electronic collars.

We acquired the proper electronic bark collars and had the dogs wear them battery free for a week. This exercise would hopefully keep the dogs from getting "Collar smart", meaning that they would not realize that the collar was providing the correction. I advised the owners that when the dogs started barking they were to go out and position themselves between the dog and the threat place, an open palm over the muzzle of the dog and say, "Enough!". After the week was up the owners were to re-install the batteries and monitor the dogs the first few times they barked. This would ensure that there were no adverse affects from the collars.

Reports back from the owners indicate the process worked extremely well and that the dogs have quieted down considerably with no more HOA fines due to excessive barking.

CHAPTER 8
POSSESSIONS

POSSESSION IS 9/10THS OF THE LAW

I've always been fascinated how and why dogs initiate play with toys. I've often wondered what makes them pick their toys like an old sock, stuffed toy, or a piece of wood. Is it the shape? Is it the texture? Or is it the scent? At what point do some dogs become very possessive over the toy to the point of aggression? In rescue we see possession aggression take two forms; food based or toy (trophy) based. Both types of aggression are systemic forms of dominance. The dogs believe that they are high ranking members of the pack and as such either the food or the toy belongs to them and only them. Any attempt to remove the item is seen from the dog's perspective as a direct challenge to its position in the pack.

An interesting behavior that I've noted on several occasions is dogs that love to dash off with a piece of the owners clothing. The article of clothing can range from a lone sock to an article of underwear. The question becomes why? Scent is usually what motivates a dog to select a particular item. Dog's think with their noses and no matter how many times we wash our clothes there is still our lingering scent on them. When our dog's dash off with an article of ours with our scent on it they have in their minds secured a "kill". A dominant trait for sure, inevitably left unchecked our dogs would accumulate enough "kills" to build a trophy pile.

This same behavior has been observed in wild packs. In the wild a pack will have a trophy pile made up of bones, sticks, or other unique objects acquired during the pack's adventures. The Alphas have complete ownership of the trophy pile and any pack member that wants an item must seek approval from the Alphas. Any pack member violating this protocol is severely dealt with. Consider this, a common mistake that most new dog owners make is that they will run off to a local pet store and purchase several toys and basket to place them in. Upon return home from the store they will present the toy basket ("Trophy pile") to the dog. By giving the dog its' own trophy pile you just told it, it is a high ranking member of the pack and if we want a toy we will check with them first.

This leads to one of the tenants of our program guidelines that during the initial boot camp period of establishing the Alpha your dog is allowed one action toy. That toy can be anything of your choosing but only comes out when you decide its playtime and is put away when you decide playtime is over. Whatever the toy make sure that you win the game every time. If the item is a tug toy you have to win the tug of war every time. Alphas are typically the smartest, strongest, and fastest of the pack and by winning each game (contest) you're reinforcing the point with your dog that you are the Alpha.

In general this systematic approach works very well in establishing Alpha over time, but what does one do when faced with unexpected possession aggression? Imagine approaching your dog only to have it growl or snarl at you as a form of warning. This is the moment of truth and depending on how you react will determine the type of relationship you will forge with your dog. Will you become the Alpha or will you be viewed as a subordinate member of the pack? What are the consequences if you react badly? Most often the worst aspect of the situation is how it catches us off guard.

Well run rescue groups typically perform a temperament test prior to adopting out a dog so that new owners are made aware of any problematic possession issues. This information is invaluable and can provide the new owner with some foresight that they can react properly when faced with an act of possession aggression. Unfortunately temperament tests are not a guarantee that dogs won't show possession aggression later. Dogs that are highly dominant with aggressive tendencies will often show possession aggression during temperament tests. It is the seemingly docile dogs that lack self confidence that will never show possession aggression during a temperament test that can later become possession aggressive.

A general rule I've adopted over the years is that anytime you approach a dog huddled over a possession be prepared for some form of aggression. The key thing to remember is that if your dog growls or snarls causing you to back off you just took two huge steps backward in forging an Alpha relationship with your dog. The rule here is that you can not back down if your dog challenges you by snarling or growling. You have to take charge of the situation. The question for the owner becomes how should I react?

My first piece of advice is not to grab the dog's collar for two reasons. First by reaching towards a snarling dog using your hands you have a pretty good chance of getting bit. Second we want to teach dogs that hands are a good thing and only used for petting, not for correction. Now that leaves us with how to correct the dog for the bad behavior. If by chance you have your dog on leash and collar you've got a great opportunity to teach your dog proper behavior. Begin by grasping the end of the leash applying a quick snap coinciding with a firm "NO". The instant your dog stops the offending behavior and makes eye contact give him or her positive praise, "Good Dog!"

Most of us don't keep our dogs on a leash 24/7 unless we are trying to modify a behavior. So if this is the case then you will have to give a verbal correction (with a slight modification). Do the following; a loud "NO" followed by grasping your dogs back legs and lifting upward. Once your dog is upside down and has dropped the possession dish out loads of positive praise. What we are accomplishing here is defusing the situation by correction, distraction, and refocus. Doing so your dog will less likely attack because he or she won't see your actions as a threat. To ultimately solve the problem get the dog on a leash and recreate the circumstances that led to the possession aggression so that you can deliver a leash correction. Following this technique can go along way in getting the behavior corrected. In severe cases I recommend consulting with a professional dog trainer or behaviorist.

CASE STUDY: BITE THE HAND THAT FEEDS

I recently received a call from a local rescue group about an eighteen-month-old beagle named "Bailey". Bailey had begun to show signs of extreme food aggression. The aggression had become so bad that no-one could move about the kitchen when he started to eat. Bailey had been adopted by a young married couple some sixteen weeks earlier with no indications of food aggression. Bailey had been a stray and very emaciated when turned into rescue. After spending two weeks in foster care Bailey had been adopted by the young couple.

I began the evaluation by reviewing our program guidelines starting with the sleep location followed by the feeding routine. Fortunately the couple had been having Bailey sleep in the kennel at night with no issues. Their feeding routine lacked discipline. They had simply just fed Bailey without making him wait for the "OK". I reviewed with them the proper technique in feeding bringing Bailey into the room to demonstrate. I could instantly see the wife's hesitation in me doing so thinking that I would be attacked by Bailey. Prior to bringing Bailey into the house I had performed the threshold technique (swinging the door open and closed) not allowing him to enter before me. I then placed him on lead and collar outside delivering a snap correction when he tried to walk ahead of me dominating him and letting him know who was in charge. Needless to say when I demonstrated the feeding routine Bailey presented no problems. This told me immediately that Bailey had not accepted the young married couple as the Alpha pair.

At this point I needed more information so I asked the couple, " … at what point did Bailey start to show signs of aggression ?" The wife told me that after having Bailey for about three weeks he had started to show subtle signs of being possessive and aggressive about food. The first instance of aggression was when the wife had approached Bailey during feeding to add some cooked carrots to his food bowl only to be greeted with a low growl. Once she heard the growl she immediately backed off. I informed her that she had backed down from a challenge which only fueled more food aggression from Bailey. She went on to tell me that a week or so later she had been walking past Bailey during feeding only to see him snarl and growl. From that point forward Bailey would eat in the kitchen while the wife either left the room or remained perfectly still.

A couple of elements were coming together to set the stage for Bailey's food aggression. First Bailey showed aggression at the three week mark. This is the point in time where dogs determine that where they have been sleeping in the same house with the other pets and humans now form the pack that they are a member of. Bailey had showed the wife food aggression and the wife had backed off. This gave Bailey his first indication that he was a high ranking member of the pack.

Second as a stray Bailey had been emaciated and most likely had to fight for every meal. Over the course of the past few weeks Bailey had been putting on weight and getting stronger. Dogs that are weak will not attempt to ascend to Alpha status because they know that they are at a severe disadvantage. Bailey had turned the corner physically and with the perceived lack of Alpha in his pack it was his responsibility to ascend to the role. So as for feeding time Bailey assumed that all food was his and as Alpha he would never allow himself to become weak and emaciated as before. So when the wife or anyone else approached the food bowl Bailey would in no uncertain terms let them know he was the Alpha.

I was certain that Bailey's food aggression could be corrected being that I was able to demonstrate the feeding routine without incident. After reviewing the program guidelines the couple agreed that the items made sense and were not negotiable. The program guideline items would be followed to the letter, key point being to remain calm, confident, and consistent. I am happy to report after implementing the program guidelines over the course of a few weeks that Bailey has showed no more food aggression.

CASE STUDY: TROPHIES

A few months ago I received an urgent call from the owner of a rescued Boxer named Bowser. There had been some sort of altercation between Bowser and the resident Boxer named Jesse. The owner went on to explain that three weeks prior to the incident neither Jesse nor Bowser had shown any aggression towards each other during their initial introduction. In fact just after a few minutes both dogs were off running and playing as though they were litter mates. The owner couldn't understand why both dogs had gotten into such a bad fight as to cause a trip to the vet's office. Fortunately just a few stitches were required to repair the damage. One could not say the same for the owners frayed nerves.

The incident had occurred in the kitchen while Jesse had been chewing on a favorite tug toy. Bowser had entered the room and was passing by a few feet from Jesse when the fight started. The owner had stepped in trying to stop the fight by grabbing Bowser's collar only to be greeted with a bite. Unable to break-up the fight the dogs eventually wore themselves out and stopped. Not knowing what to do the owner kept both dogs separated.

The owner's initial inclination was to return Bowser to rescue thinking that Jesse wasn't the problem. I've heard this comment on more than one occasion. My reply provides the owner food for thought, "So you've decided to be a one dog family." Responding to the owners' inquisitive look I go on to explain that the environment creates the dog and left unchecked could have the same results when introducing a new dog later. I told the owner that now is the time to correct the problem so that he could enjoy both dogs.

The owner agreed and we decided an in-home consultation was the next step. In the meantime the owner would reunite the dogs (minus toys). During the home visit both dogs were to remain outside on the patio while we reviewed the process for establishing Alpha. For the most part the dogs were very well behaved and after a few minutes both owner and I stepped outside onto the patio. I continued to talk with the owner ignoring the dogs until they had been calm for five minutes. What happened next caught me completely by surprise.

After petting both dogs I asked the owner to get their leashes ready. As the owner pulled out the leashes Jesse stood up on his hind legs and engaged Bowser in a display of dominance wrapping both paws around his neck. Bowser stood up responded in kind and now both dogs were on their hind legs with their front paws wrapped around each other snarling. Before either of us could react we had an all out dog fight on our hands. To make matters worse the patio was fairly small enclosed area surrounded by three walls, so breaking up the dog fight would be difficult. My biggest concern was the owner who in a state of panic kept screaming at the dogs and trying to reach in to grab the collar. I kept reminding the owner, "Don't reach for their collars, they will bite you." Quickly I formed a loop with my leash and attempted to lasso a dog. My first and second attempts failed, but the third try was successful in roping a hind leg.

I wasn't sure which dog I had lassoed but in a fast single motion I lifted the hind legs off the ground while reaching behind me to open the sliding glass door. The strategy worked as Bowser bounded into the house with me slamming the door closed behind him. With the dogs finally separated the owner lamented how badly Bowser had behaved. I quickly pointed out that from my perspective Jesse had begun the posturing and displayed at least a half dozen signs of dominance before the altercation began. Catching my breath I went on to say, "… if we are to assign blame then the Alpha is responsible for the fight occurring." Owner responded, "So you're saying Jesse is to blame here?" Slowly and deliberately I stated, "Not exactly, you are." This was an epiphany for the owner; I went on to explain that if your dogs fight in your presence they don't view you as Alpha in charge. Bewildered the owner said, "I've had other foster dogs here prior to Bowser's arrival with no problems". I could see that the owner still wasn't convinced that Bowser was not the culprit. My next question, "What are you doing different today then when the foster dogs were staying here?" The owner pondered for a minute and then got this sort of half guilty look on his face, "Since Bowser arrival I haven't kenneled Jesse at night letting him sleep wherever he wants."

This was a huge revelation and almost immediately after saying it the owner realized what he had been doing wrong by stating, "By letting Jesse sleep wherever he wanted to I was sending him mixed signals on his position in the pack." My next statement was going to be critical. I told the owner, "It takes twelve weeks to establish the Alpha and you have to remain calm, consistent, and confident the entire time. Once you've established the Alpha and there is a change in the household such as a new person or a move you have to do an abbreviated version of establishing Alpha for about three weeks." The owner agreed. We laid out a plan that for the next three weeks the dogs would be in boot camp mode following the program guideline to the letter. I am glad to report that after a few weeks there have been no further signs of aggression from either dog.

CHAPTER 9
BONDING

A Dog's Devotion

There has always been something magical about the bonds that form between canine and human. I have often pondered about what emotions dogs and humans have in common and what part do emotions play in forming those bonds.

The simplest place to begin the examination is to observe how our dogs interact with us when we first adopt them into our homes. I've always been fascinated by how dogs react when they first are placed in homes with children. Like a moth to flame most dogs immediately gravitate to the smallest of the children to begin the socialization process. I have often observed the same socialization process at dog parks. Ultimately when a new dog enters the park it will head to a group of dogs and pick out the smaller of the dogs in stature to socialize with first. The dog will quickly move from one dog to the next in stature continuing to socialize. Once the greeting ritual is complete the group is off running and playing until the next new dog enters the park starting the ritual all over again.

One keen observation can be made here, in the canine world *size matters*. That said; is the basis for all canine human relationships rooted in dominance (size based)? Do dogs simply start at the lowest point of the food chain and work their way up? Once the dog has determined who it can dominate do we mistake that bond as devotion or love? In turn, when we establish Alpha with our dogs should we interpret that bond as loyalty? I have often wondered these things and have come to the conclusion that the bond formed between canines and humans is very complex. In this relationship between canines and humans one has to be dominant. When we choose to be dominant the bond forged is undeniably love, devotion, and loyalty. When our dogs are allowed to dominate, the relationship becomes subservient where we are simply a subordinate member of the pack that has use as a food dispenser or door opener. In the years that I've worked with dogs I am convinced that when we as humans establish the Alpha with our dogs they live happier and longer lives.

CASE STUDY: WHAT HAVE YOU DONE TO MY KID?

I received a call from a distressed mother that had adopted a Boxer named Mika some 3 months earlier. The mother was very concerned because over the past month or so Mika had lost about fifteen percent of her body weight. Mika had had a full workup by a local veterinarian where nothing was discovered that could explain the sudden weight loss From a physical standpoint Mika was in perfect health. The perplexing problem was that despite the weight loss Mika would eat only sporadically with consistent diarrhea. By the sounds of it, this had to be a physiological problem. I was sure that this would turn out to be a health problem and not related to any sort of behavioral issue.

As part of each evaluation we capture the family structure to determine what sort of dynamics might come into play when we start the process of establishing the Alpha. In this case there were two adults and a thirteen year old teenager named Montgomery. In each evaluation we discuss how important sleep location is and how important it is in establishing Alpha with the dog. In this case the dog had been sleeping in the kennel in Montgomery's bedroom. The mother went on to tell me that they had followed all the program guidelines that they had received from the local rescue group when they adopted Mika and that all had gone well. The mother explained that Mika and Montgomery had been nearly inseparable and that their only time apart was when Montgomery was away at school for the day. It seemed very strange to me that Mika was under such stress with no clear indicator as to why. The answer to my next question gave me a starting point.

I asked the mother what had changed over the past few weeks, was there any stress in the family? She thought for a moment and told me that about six weeks earlier Montgomery had become very ill and had to stay home for a few days from school. She said that when she went to check on him in his bedroom she would find him sleeping on the floor with his fingers poked through the kennel door so as to touch Mika. Every time his mother had Montgomery return to bed he would complain always managing to get back on the bedroom floor along side Mika's kennel. On the doctor's advice the mother moved the kennel down to the family room so as to remove the opportunity for Montgomery to sleep on the floor. The result was that Montgomery wound up on the family room couch so that he could again poke his fingers into Mika's kennel.

Being close to Mika seemed to do the trick and after a few days Montgomery was fit as a fiddle. To get things back to normal Mika's kennel was moved back into Montgomery's room. Things didn't get quite back to normal; Mika decided that unless Montgomery slept close to her kennel she was going to make a fuss until he complied. Montgomery being your typical teenager decided that sleep was a priority and that Mika could sleep in her kennel downstairs in the family room where if she made noise it would be of no consequence.

Initially the mother had not connected the two events because the weight loss had happened over several weeks, but as we both discussed the matter further we both agreed that this was the catalyst. Now the question remained; what would be the remedy? In this case the program guidelines for establishing the Alpha had been followed to the letter so why then was Mika continuing to believe she was responsible for Montgomery? The answer lay in the way in which Mika and Montgomery interacted on daily basis. Being that Mika and Montgomery were inseparable the next step was to see how they spent their time together.

As one would expect any teenager to do in this electronic age Montgomery spent a lot of time lounging around on the family room floor playing video games. Naturally Mika would spend most of her time lying on the floor right next to Montgomery on the same physical plane. When Montgomery got up to do his homework Mika would follow and promptly place her head on top of Montgomery's feet under the desk. Finally anytime Montgomery went outside to skate board or ride his bike Mika would faithfully pull Montgomery along. Based on these interactions it was pretty clear that Mika had taken on the responsibility of Montgomery as being hers. Playing on the same physical plane, allowing Mika to herd Montgomery by resting her head on his feet, to allowing her to lead the hunt by pulling him on skateboard or bike were all key indicators to Mika that she was a higher ranking member of the pack than Montgomery. Montgomery returned to health and Mika was no longer able to protect him from daily concerns she had gone neurotic to the point of ill health.

Now that we knew the reason, the next step was to set Montgomery in charge of Mika. Being that the family was already following the program guidelines used to establish Alpha the quickest method to gaining control of Mika and establishing dominance was to hand the leash to Montgomery and have them go through the paces of a basic obedience program. In addition to the basic obedience program we had Montgomery perform the feeding ritual with Mika insuring that she eats. Also no playing video games from the family room floor or allowing Mika to rest her head on his feet while doing homework. I am happy to report that after just a couple of weeks of basic obedience training Mika was on the mend and putting on weight again.

CASE STUDY: JEKYLL AND HYDE

How quickly can a dog bond to a human? Is it instantaneous or does it take some time? Is instantaneous bonding canine-human subservient relationship or human master? It is fascinating to try to wrap ones head around such questions. This case study involves a young Boxer male named Diesel who within the first 48 hours of adoption showed some extreme aggression.

Diesel had been turned over to rescue by a young single woman who at the time was living alone in an apartment. According to the woman Diesel was a good dog, but due to his large size and the apartment being small the woman felt it best to find a better home for him. This is a common story for most dogs turned over to rescue so nothing seemed out of the ordinary. A local Boxer rescue group received Diesel, performed a temperament test to find no possession aggression, human aggression, or dog-on-dog aggression. Diesel spent the next couple of months in rescue getting along splendidly with three other foster Boxers.

The day came right before the Christmas holidays for Diesel to be adopted to a family with two young children, a four year old daughter and a son barely past the age of one. The parents wanted to surprise their four year old daughter at Christmas. The family went through the normal application process and were screened coming back as the perfect home. So Christmas Eve arrived and the couple set out to pick up Diesel. Upon meeting Diesel the wife described to me later that it seemed as though he instantly bonded to her. At the initial introduction he wouldn't take his eyes from her and constantly wanted to be at her side, paying little or no attention to the husband. My initial thought was this was sort of unusual, but more then likely when they got him home he would gravitate towards the children.

Upon arriving home that evening and surprising the four year old daughter Diesel's focus was still on the wife, never leaving her side or being out of eyeshot. This struck me as even more unusual in that Diesel seemed to pretty much ignore the rest of the family members that were there visiting for the holidays. Somewhat unprepared and not having a crate for Diesel to sleep in the first night, the wife decided she would sleep on the living room couch with Diesel resting on the floor nearby. Upon looking back I told the wife that this had been a bad idea from the start. Even though this was still early in the acclamation period it sent Diesel a very strong signal that he was high ranking member of the pack.

The next morning being Christmas there was a lot of commotion with family members and children opening gifts. All the while Diesel remained close to the wife never leaving her side, nor taking his eyes away from her. At one point during the morning's festivities the four year old daughter had crawled up onto the Mother's lap unwrapping a gift. As the gift was opened the Mother began bouncing her leg as most parents have a habit of doing. Well Diesel must have taken this as sign that the Mother wanted her Daughter off her lap and promptly nipped the Daughter in the face leaving a couple of bruises. Horrified the mother placed Diesel outside for the rest of the morning.

Diesel seemed to be fine in the backyard simply staring in at the activities through the sliding glass door never letting his gaze stray to far from the wife. After a couple of hours the couple determined that it must have been a fluke and that they should let Diesel back into the house to be with his new family. Immediately Diesel was at the wife's side not leaving her for a moment. Then something bad happened, as the wife explained it to me later she wasn't sure but Diesel gave a low growl to the

Mother-in-law that alarmed the family. I didn't ask how she got along with the Mother-in-law but if I had to guess on the surface it may have seemed pleasant enough, but there might have been some underlying tension that Diesel picked up on. None the less the growl warranted another expulsion to the backyard were again Diesel contently peered in through the sliding glass door at the wife.

Later that afternoon it came time for the family to depart for some planned activities. Feeling somewhat guilty about Diesel's predicament the wife decided to spend a few minutes with Diesel out in the backyard before leaving. As it came time to leave the wife was situated with Diesel at the far end of the yard when the Husband emerged through the Arcadia door motioning and calling to his wife in a loud voice that it was time to leave. Almost instantaneously Diesel was in a full sprint heading towards the husband hackles raised and barking furiously. Shocked the husband retreated back through the Arcadia door closing it behind him to see Diesel leap from ten feet hitting the Arcadia door in mid air. Unfazed Diesel promptly circled around trying to get through a window at the husband. The family couldn't take the risk of injury to the children and what seemed to be a problem had escalated to an all out emergency.

It was some hours later that evening when I was able to communicate with the wife directly. I reviewed the incidence and explained to her why it had not been a good idea to have Diesel sleep in the living room the first night. To my amazement she was committed to work with Diesel because he had bonded with her so strongly. This was an usual case in a couple of respects, one in particular was the short time it took to bond. In most cases there is little history on dogs turned into rescue and it is not unusual for original owners to hide the truth about the dog to make sure it is not rejected by the rescue group. In this case all we knew was that a single young woman turned the dog over stating that she had no issues. Upon investigating we found out the woman and the wife could have passed off as sisters if not twins. Physical characteristics have a lot to do with how dogs associate people or in some cases bad people. In this case it was obvious that Diesel had bonded to the wife so quickly because he was reminded of his previous owner. But what was the reason for the assault on the husband?

In working through Diesel's background we attempted to contact the former owner to ask her if there had been any issues like this before. Attempts like this are usually pointless because people are afraid that they may be in trouble for being less then truthful about their previous pets, in this case the woman had moved making information gathering more difficult. We later learned that previous owner had been in abusive relationship with her boyfriend and from Diesel's reaction to the husband it must have been pretty violent. Violent to the point were the woman could have spent time in the hospital. Either way these events in Diesel's previous home had traumatized him. Imagine when Diesel saw the husband coming through the Arcadia door motioning to his wife in a load voice that Christmas morning. Remember dogs don't understand language but recognize words so from Diesel's point of view it appeared that there was going to be another assault on his master. Based on Diesel's reaction this was going to be unequivocally unacceptable, hence the reason for the assault against the husband. Understandable, but not acceptable under any terms.

Not all case studies have a happy ending, in some cases they never end at all but remain works in progress. Canines that have trauma rooted this deep can sometimes take a lifetime to correct. I can tell you that following the process staying calm, confident, and consistent provides the best chance for rehabilitation. Canine's lives, emotions, and behaviors are very fluid and one can never assume that once a behavior is corrected that it might not resurface. The key is to understand the root cause and by consistent behavior modification technique can effect a change for the better. In Diesel's case it will have to be constant awareness and monitoring to make sure that Dr. Jekyll doesn't become Mr. Hyde.

CHAPTER 10
AGRESSION
LOVE HATE RELATIONSHIP

One of the biggest concerns facing rescue groups today is the rehabilitation and placement of aggressive dogs. These dogs present a liability and are very hard to place in new homes. The adopters have to be willing to work with the dog in modifying aggressive behavior while maintaining a tough love mentality. This goes against the whole grain of adoption in general for it is human nature to adopt rescued dogs because of a soft spot in the heart. Many rescue groups have a process in place that identifies aggressive dogs and properly matches them with the right adopters. These rescue groups have set up support systems so that adopters can get help if the dog becomes a problem. Understanding the root cause and types of aggressive behavior is important in modifying the behavior.

Uninformed people choosing the wrong breed and loving them into aggression creates the classic profile of the aggressive rescue dog. It is ninety percent environmental factors and ten percent genetics (breeding) that form the personality of a dog with no two dogs being exactly alike. Breeds inherently have characteristics that tend to make the dog more spirited, dominant, and confident such as American Bulldogs, Bull Terriers, Boxers, and Doberman Pinchers to mention a few. In most cases people choose the type of dog as a symbol or an extension of their own personalities. Not soon after getting these dogs do the new owners begin to realize that they have more then they can handle. On average these dogs never see their first year in the homes before being handed over to rescue.

The first signs of aggressive behavior (nips or bites) will surface during first few confrontations between owner and canine. It is how we react to these confrontations that will set the tone for our relationship with our canines. If we back down from the initial challenge (confrontation) it will only encourage dominant behavior to continue leading to dominance based aggression (see Aggression Chart depicted later in chapter). On the other hand if the owner overreacts causing the dog to lash back the canine may develop fear based aggression. Identifying the type of aggression dictates the type of behavior modification needed to correct the behavior. For dominant based aggression confrontation and correction is the best method to correct aggression. For fear based aggression, correction followed by confidence building works best in correcting aggression while overcoming the canine's fears.

Dealing with dominance based aggression can be the most physically demanding and dangerous behavior to correct. Draw a mental picture of the school yard bully and correlate it to the dominant canine, "I am stronger and faster than you so therefore I'll have my way with you. Try anything I will growl or worse yet bite you". Most of us learned at an early age the best way to deal with a school yard bully is to confront them head on. Avoiding the bully or trying reason with them never really gets us very far. Dealing with confrontation head on, finding the courage to overcome builds our character. It is much the same way when confronting a dominant aggressive canine.

Determining the trigger for aggression is the key. Note the Aggression Chart depicted later in this chapter. The trigger for dominance based aggression can be traced back to an object rather than an event. Food, possession, or prey drive objects can trigger a dominant based aggressive act. Delivering a severe correction to the offender at the instant the aggression begins is the best way to modify the behavior. Much like dealing with a school yard bully a direct punch in the face sends the appropriate message to a human, but what about our canines? Verbal corrections due little to modify aggressive behavior and in some cases incite the dog into a full out attack.

The first point of the exercise is to have complete control of the environment. One must maintain control via leash and chain collar while introducing the trigger object (e.g. possession, another dog, human, etc.). The instant the aggression begins a level three correction of lifting the front legs off the ground and holding the position until the canine's back legs relax sends the appropriate message, "Your behavior is absolutely unequivocally unacceptable, as Alpha I will correct you." It has been my experience that in most cases one might have to deliver two to three corrections over the first couple of weeks before convincing the offending canine that aggression is futile.

On more than one occasion I have been asked, "What is a person to do if an aggressive dog comes running up to us in the open?" Naturally the scenario always has no place of retreat or ad-hoc weapons available for use to fend off the attack. I've had success in the past with what I call the invisible dog technique. What you do is take a non-threatening posture and as the dog approaches look a few feet to the right and start speaking in a high voice to an invisible dog. Tell the invisible dog, "You're absolutely the best dog on the planet…" In most cases the aggressive dog will stop dead in its tracks and look at you as if you've lost your mind. Keep in mind that you're assuming a non-threatening position and attempting to distract the approaching canine. Eventually the dog will either walk up to you in a non-threatening manner or simply loose interest and run off in another direction. This technique also works great for catching stray dogs that are hesitant to come to you.

Fear based aggression requires a slightly different tact. One needs to correct the bad behavior while building the canine's confidence. The basis for fear based aggression is the fight or flight mentality. Given the opportunity most canines will choose flight, but it is those few when cornered that choose to fight which characterize fear based aggression. Correcting fear based aggression is a much longer process than correcting dominance based aggression. In order to modify fear based aggression one must establish Alpha with the canine first (12 weeks). Doing so insures that the canine looks to the Alpha to acknowledge threats. To correct this behavior we must expose the canine to the trigger object while taking no notice (in other words not acknowledging the threat). The instant the aggression begins a quick correction (level 1) followed by immediate positive praise sends the message that I as the Alpha am responsible for dealing with the threat and not the subordinate members of the pack. Over a few weeks of repeatedly correcting fear based aggression followed by immediate positive praise will correct the problem in most cases.

There is debate amongst the dog community in regards to a term known as "Redirected Aggression". Many organizations have accepted the term to characterize aggression that occurs when a canine is provoked while unable to attack a passing intruder by redirecting aggression onto a nearby person or animal. For example, a person or animal passing nearby incites a group of dogs behind a fence that may turn and attack each other because they can't reach the intruder. On the surface this seems to be a reasonable explanation, however upon close examination it doesn't hold up. I've seen this behavior on several occasions and the first thing I notice before any aggression occurs between the dogs is a posturing ritual. The dominant dogs begin to physically posture amongst each other as if to say, "I will greet the approaching intruder as a high ranking member of the pack." It is when one of the other pack members decides that they won't be an accomplice that the dog fighting begins. The key point is that if the fighting occurs in your presence then the dogs have not accepted you as Alpha. When your gone all bets are off as to what will happen if another intruder were to pass by. Whether or not another dog fight breaks out will depend on how strong of a dominant trait each dog has.

An interesting comment I have heard from dog owners on several occasions is that their dogs somehow form grudges and given the opportunity will seek revenge on an offender for losing a previous skirmish. To prove the point they note that their dogs only fight three or four times a year. This sentiment absolutely confounds me and I am quick to illustrate to the owners if the dogs are fighting it's your fault as owner not the dog. We can equate some human emotions with canine emotions, but those emotions that rely on time (such as revenge) we should not. Again canines live in the here and now and when they do fight it is a result of dominant posturing to be a high ranking member of the pack and as Alpha we can never allow this to take place.

We also have to approach the correction of these aggressive behaviors from a time based view. Dogs don't understand punishment, but do understand corrections. I've had a few people tell me that when their dog does something inappropriate they are sent to their time out corner as though they were children. The owners always tell me that the dog looks dejected and knows why it is being punished. This notion could not be farther from the truth. After a few moments in the time out the dog no longer remembers why it's there lending this sort of behavior modification technique to confuse dogs that lack confidence. Again effective behavior modification is to correct the dog the instant the unwanted behavior begins followed immediately with positive praise once the offending behavior has stopped. The key is to remember to apply corrections not punishment.

In aggression unwanted behavior normally takes the form of a nip or a bite. In some cases the nip or bite is preceded by a warning growl. There are signs to look for that will indicate that the dog is getting ready to bite. Dogs that have stopped panting, become semi rigid with eyes focused are prepared to bite. Once we recognize the warning signs the most important thing to remember is not to back down, but be prepared to apply a level two or three correction immediately. Most people have a lot of trepidation when faced with the possibility of getting bit. I remind them that as long as you have control of the dog via leash and chain collar you're being presented with a golden opportunity to teach the dog a well valued lesson. In my experience at most two or three corrections are needed with the overly aggressive dominant dogs to get the behavior corrected.

The public doesn't really distinguish between nips and bites. In the public eye they are all classified as a bite as is the case with most local animal control bureaus, but for our purposes it useful to distinguish the two. In general nips are corrections that dogs will perform on a human for what it deems is inappropriate behavior. The root cause for a nip can be either fear based aggression or dominant based aggression. A bite is characterized by a dog latching on and shaking indicating very dominant aggressive behavior. My stance has been that dogs that nip almost always can be rehabilitated. Dogs that are beyond rehabilitation are ones that go from "zero-to-bite" with no indication. These are potentially dangerous dogs of which I have encountered less then a half a dozen. I call these dogs as being "Hard wired" wrong and regrettably beyond rehabilitation.

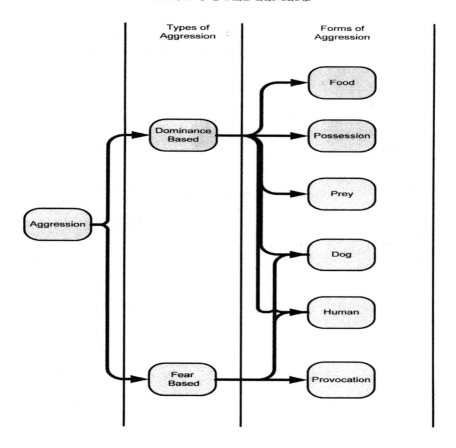

CASE STUDY: THE RELUCTANT DEFENDER

Not all dogs that come under our care and guidance come by way of rescue groups. On occasion we come across dogs in every day circumstances in which we take a personal interest. This case is about a young six-month-old Border Collie named Harlie that we happened to meet on a ranch in Northern California. Harlie had been adopted as a six-week-old puppy by a young couple who were residing in an apartment. The wife was a school teacher spending the majority of the day away from home while the Husband worked at a local ranch. As a young pup Harlie would play with the couple's young daughter for a few minutes each day. Feeling guilty about the amount of time Harlie was spending alone at the apartment the husband began bringing Harlie to the ranch during the work day. As time wore on and Harlie grew it became more difficult to keep her confined at night in the apartment. So more often than not it became a rare event that Harlie would spend the night at apartment. Harlie would find himself confined to the ranch office for up to 12 hours a day only to be let out when the husband arrived for the work day.

We went to meet Harlie and the husband one day at the ranch during a visit. The husband took an interest in our dog training experience commenting that he was having nothing but trouble with his 6 month old Border Collie. In fact things had gotten so out of hand that Harlie had nipped several people leading to the fear that eventually there would be a serious attack. At this point he was seriously considering euthanizing Harlie. We spoke at length about our methods and program and how it could help Harlie overcome what appeared to be fear based aggression. The husband listened intently and was willing to make an attempt at rehabilitating Harlie agreeing that Harlie would be spending nights back at the apartment in a kennel per our program guidelines. We scheduled our first session together a few days later.

The first session with Harlie was a definite eye opener. Coaxing her out of the ranch office was nearly impossible. Harlie's fear was so overwhelming for her that she was lashing out at anything within striking distance. It became so bad that during the walk with me stop with me exercise she tried no less then seven times to bite. Each attempt was met with a level three correction followed up with immediate praise. The husband was absolutely beside himself convinced that there was no hope for Harlie. We rarely see cases this severe so we agreed that there would need to be daily confidence building sessions, with Harlie spending each night at the apartment in her kennel.

Over the next few sessions Harlie had only improved marginally still attempting to bite if given the opportunity. Arriving early one cold winter morning we discovered Harlie locked in the office with no sign of the husband. A few minutes later with a rather embarrassed look on his face the husband came strolling up the gravel driveway. When asked what had happened and more importantly why hadn't Harlie spent the night at the apartment he confessed that Harlie had not spent a single night there. Absolutely flabbergasted the point was made that Harlie had no connection to him other than him coming into the office as the human food dispenser and that Harlie as a young puppy had been left as the reluctant defender of the den. No wonder she was fearful of everything and everyone. To make matters worse it was discovered that the husband had attempted to control Harlie's aggression by using a prong collar.

Confronted with the evidence of border line abuse we convinced the husband to give up Harlie. Harlie was placed in a normal home setting with one of our trainers. After several weeks of intense behavior modification and basic obedience training Harlie no longer has any aggression issues and is ready to be a certified therapy dog.

CASE STUDY: THE BULLY PULPIT

This case study involves a gorgeous two and half year old petite Boxer named "Roxy" and an eighteen month old brut of a Boxer mix named "Logan". The owners had had Roxy since a puppy with her topping out at 45 lbs when Logan was brought into the household as a young pup. From day one Roxy had done what we have probably all seen other older female dogs do with puppies and that is pounce on them, roll them around or otherwise physically dominate them with hard play. This sort of posturing play had continued without incident until recently when it appears that Logan now weighing over 90 lbs (nearly double the weight of Roxy) had had enough and decided to retaliate causing Roxy several stitches. The owners were absolutely distraught when they had contacted the local Boxer rescue group convinced that one of the dogs had to go. Upon contacting the owners and after discussing the situation they were more then willing to try anything to correct the problem and not have to split up the dogs. The last thing they wanted was to have to give up one of the dogs to rescue.

The owners lived in a modest home and upon entering I noticed that the interior of the home had recently been remodeled with new back room additions to the house. Both dogs had been sequestered separately, Roxy in the backyard and Logan locked in a back bedroom as is the routine during an initial consultation so neither dog could greet me upon my entering the home. I made sure that I did not knock or ring the doorbell but rather called from my cell phone at the front door to let the owners know that I had arrived. This is a technique I use on initial consultation, after all an Alpha would never knock or ring a door bell prior to entering the den. This technique lends itself to dogs remaining quiet during the ensuing twenty-minute conversation reviewing Alpha principles as was the case during this consultation.

In looking for a triggering event to the aggression I asked the question, "Did the problems start around the time of the remodel?" Both owners paused for a moment and with an astonished look on their faces stated yes. I went on to explain that anytime there is a change in either the pack structure or the den it is complete chaos for the dogs and they look to see if the Alpha leadership should change. In this case Roxy had been the Alpha and Logan having reached his prime was no longer going to accept that Roxy, half his weight, would remain Alpha of the pack. After all as is with all dogs, size matters. We continued reviewing the Alpha elements (e.g. sleeping location, feeding routine, etc.) with the owners becoming pretty discouraged stating that it appears that they had done just about everything wrong up to this point. I mentioned that the purpose of the consultation and evaluation was not to point out what they were doing wrong necessarily but to flip things to the dog's perspective in order to educate the owners.

As the conversation continued I asked the owners to describe what they see as the major problems with their dogs starting with Roxy. Without hesitation both owners stated that Roxy was the instigator. In every fight that had ensued Roxy had attacked Logan first by jumping on him. In one case when they tried to break up the fight Roxy had nipped one of the owners on the hand. I asked them if they had reached in for the collar when this happened and both stated emphatically yes. I reviewed with them that hands are not weapons and should never be used to grab a dog's collar for correction and that if ever presented with a dog fight grab the back legs of the dog to pull them apart. I emphasized that it is better to stay away from the "business" end of the dog when trying to break up a fight. I was starting to get the impression very quickly that if one of the dogs had to go, it would be Roxy. Note that during this whole conversation Roxy had been peering in at me through the sliding glass door perfectly behaved. We continued out into the backyard where I performed a physical assessment on Roxy with absolutely no issues. From what I could see Roxy was a perfectly behaved dog. I asked the owners to put Roxy back in and bring Logan into the backyard while we remained inside discussing his behavior issues.

To hear the owners describe Logan's behavior around them one would think he was a perfectly behaved dog and at a glance, with him peering at me through the sliding glass door it seemed so. I noticed that the owners seemed to be avoiding the subject of Logan's behavior around visitors or strangers, so I asked the question. There was a slight pause and both owners went on to describe reluctantly how when neighbors pass by the front of the house they would always cross over to the other side of the street. Apparently Logan had gotten out a couple of times during the remodel and had intimidated some of the teenage neighborhood kids to the point where he now had a reputation. To reinforce this point anytime someone would pass by the front of the house Logan would sit on the top of the couch peering out the front window barking furiously. My initial thought was they would never need to buy an alarm system with Logan around. I enquired if Logan had ever bit anyone and both owners emphatically stated "No". Logan had only come as close as backing up a couple of maintenance workers barking and growling but had never made contact. Now would come the real test, to step out into the backyard with Logan.

I approached the sliding glass door and began my interaction with Logan by opening and closing the door not allowing him to enter (e.g. threshold respect). I immediately noticed that I had a problem on my hands, Logan had stopped panting, became semi-rigid, hackles raised, and pupils fixed; all signs of a dog ready to attack. At this point I knew that I would not be able to step out onto the patio without getting attacked. I had no intentions of getting into a brawl with a 90 lb. Boxer mix with no method of control (no leash) intent on taking a hunk out of me or so I thought. We quickly moved to plan B where I had the owners go outside and get Logan on a chain collar and leash. I explained to them that I would step out onto the patio ignoring Logan with a drink in hand and begin a conversation so as to represent no threat to him.

As I stepped out onto the patio with drink in hand and was only a few seconds into the conversation when I realized that Logan was snapping and growling at my pant leg. The owner had failed to react quick enough to restrain Logan from getting to me having dropped the leash in the process. It seems that whenever an attack occurs everything moves in slow motion making it seem like a minute or two has passed when in reality only a few seconds has elapsed. As events unfolded I fully expected Logan to clamp onto my leg with me having to grab the end of the leash and perform an immediate level three correction or worse yet a level four correction (i.e. helicopter motion). As Logan was being pulled back by the owner, to my astonishment I looked down only to find a little bit of drool on my pant leg. With all the drama and to my relief, this was truly a case of a dog with a bark worse then his bite. The owners went to explain that this is as far as he has ever gone with human aggression and that their concern was the fights between Roxy and Logan.

The next step of the consultation was to get Logan and Roxy in the backyard to complete the evaluation. Both dogs had been separated since the last altercation which had been about one week ago. We made sure that both dogs had leashes on so that if a fight ensued we would be able to break it up quickly. We allowed both dogs to interact in the backyard dragging leashes on the ground. I noticed immediately that in our presence Logan began a posturing ritual with Roxy. Based on his size Logan was exercising his bully pulpit. Roxy unwilling to relinquish Alpha in turn responded aggressively in which we immediately stopped the altercation. I immediately gave both owners a sort of play-by-play analysis like one would hear during a football game of what just happened highlighting Logan's initial posturing. I explained to the owners that both dogs were engaging and that if they decided to get rid of one and if they ever adopted another dog later they would likely have the same problem. The choice was clear either fix it now or become a one dog family.

The owners were committed to resolving the problem but as with many dog owners they had expected a professional to come in and fix the problem for them quickly. The next step was to lay out their responsibilities over the course of the next twelve weeks and that success or failure was in their hands depending how well they followed the Establishing Alpha Guidelines (see appendix). I am pleased to report that after the 12 week program the dogs are no longer fighting. Logan still has command of the neighborhood teenagers but the owners want it that way and honestly who could blame them.

CHAPTER 11
PUPPY IMPRINTING
BRINGING THE BABY HOME

Dogs form their personalities between the ages of two and four months, so there are few things as rewarding then for those of us that are fortunate enough to participate in forming those personalities. Negative experiences such as a trauma during this formative time in a dog's life can lead to fear based aggression. We make it distinctly clear that any dogs in our guidance during this time in their lives have to be guarded avoiding any potentially traumatic experience. Traumatic experiences can range from a dog attack, a human beating, or being hit by a car. One can imagine several different circumstances that would characterize a traumatic event. An example I use often is one where we imagine that a 4 month old puppy in a circus was beat on a daily basis by a clown wearing a red wig. Upon reaching adulthood the dog will most likely be very fearful of any clowns wearing red wigs to the point of even attacking one on sight. This of course is an extreme example and events can be much more subtle.

Some twenty years ago we adopted a miniature dachshund named Hans. My wife having raised Irish Wolfhounds and knowing that I was terrified of dogs at that time thought it best to start with a smaller breed. During this time we had placed baby gates strategically in the hallways to limit Hans roaming about the house. On one occasion our son who was seven years old at the time was stepping over a gate with Hans standing next to him when accidentally the gate fell over pinching Hans's leg rather severely. I heard a loud yelp followed by Hans running on three legs towards me for protection. I didn't think much about it at the time because Hans seemed to recover from it okay. As I remember Hans throughout his thirteen years of life he always seemed to be very aggressive towards kids that were positioned on the other side of a gate. As I recall he was about four months old when he was hurt by the falling gate.

I am a strong advocate that puppies should not be removed from their mothers until around the eight week mark. In our experience they just seem to develop better then puppies removed earlier say at four to six weeks of age. That said once you do get the puppy home there are some very important exercises you need to start especially as the dog reaches the eight week mark.

The most important thing to remember is that between the ages of two months and four months the dog's attention span is about a nanosecond. During this time period you should focus on giving sensations that the dog should get accustomed to such as manipulating the ears, paws, and teeth. This should be done three to four times a day with the dog being placed on its back in a submissive position. At this point don't worry about correcting the dog for bad behavior or necessarily being too strict with them when it comes to housebreaking.

For housebreaking make sure you're taking the puppy out about every couple of hours of waking time and praising them when they go, nothing more, nothing less. Verbally correcting a dog at this age for soiling in the house can lead to the dog hiding to urinate in the house or worse yet eating its own feces to hide the evidence from you. This is a crucial time; make sure you housebreak the dog correctly when it reaches four months of age. My standard rule is that any dog that is healthy and four months old can be housebroken within two weeks by use of the umbilical cord technique.

Now that the dog has reached the four-month mark it is important to reinforce one point; the dog is never allowed to place its open mouth on our hands. People in general think it is cute for puppies to play bite our hands. In reality all it teaches a dog from a young age is that it is acceptable for them to place an open mouth on a human. So later in life if they decide that a human is doing something inappropriate it is okay for them to correct us by taking a bite out of us. Not acceptable. Too often then not these are the human aggressive dogs that make their way into rescue organizations.

Between the ages of four and eight months is a great time to teach canine's basic obedience. All of our service canines routinely have basic obedience down by eight months and are fully advanced off-lead trained by the time they are ten to twelve months old.

CASE STUDY: DRIVING MS. DAISY

There's an old dog trainer's lament that goes, "I *have never met a dog I couldn't train, but I've met people that couldn't be trained"*. Nothing illustrates the point more then seeing the development of two (for the most part identical) canines raised in separate environments with strikingly different results. This case study is about the tale of two dogs; Daisy and Sadie.

Daisy and Sadie were littermates that were offered up as six-week-old puppies by the owner in a local grocery store parking lot for ten dollars apiece. A rescue group volunteer happened by and asked the owner of the puppies what condition the parents were in and if the puppies had seen a veterinarian. The owner wasn't very forth coming with information and when pressed that giving out unvaccinated puppies could land him in trouble he was more then happy to turn over the lot to rescue.

The puppies were immediately placed into foster homes and nurtured until they were ready to be adopted out at the age of ten weeks. As circumstances would have it the all the puppies (six in total) were adopted out almost immediately with Sadie going to a family of four and Daisy going to single woman living in a household with four roommates. Sadie's new adoptive owners had adopted before from rescue and signed almost immediately for Puppy Imprinting training. They wanted to insure that Sadie would develop into a model canine citizen. Daisy on the other hand came to be an almost constant companion to the school teacher that adopted her. We saw Sadie on a frequent basis so we were able to track her development quite closely whereas Daisy fell off the radar screen until we received an urgent call some eight months later.

It was late at night when I received a call from the local rescue group vice president asking me to call Daisy's owner about a reported bite to the face. She told me that Daisy's owner had had some guests over and that Daisy had wondered into the room where the bite victim was sitting. The victim had been introduced to Daisy earlier and had spent several minutes petting her, but upon Daisy entering the room this time the victim went to pet her and promptly got nipped in the face. Apparently a completely unprovoked attack. The question was had this happened before.

    I contacted the owner and asked for a complete aggression history on the dog from the time she had been adopted at ten weeks old. I was told that the same thing had happened on three occasions, but the other two seemed provoked somehow. She went on to describe the first incident when she had been cornered by a roommate's boyfriend in a aggressive playful sort of way and that Daisy had nipped causing nothing more than a bruise. The second episode was also almost identical to the first except it involved a different roommate's boyfriend. What had concerned the owner the most about this incident was that it appeared that Daisy had sought out the bite victim by going into the backroom.

    The backroom was full of people clamoring about with the victim engaged in conversation. When the victim saw Daisy standing and looking in the doorway she stepped closer to pet her to be greeted with a nip in the face. The owner went on to describe how fearful Daisy seemed about everything. She would frequently cower when new guests came to visit the house and that noises caused her to hide. Obviously this was a condition that had existed for some time. It was only now that symptoms were starting to emerge as fear biting had caught the attention of the owner.

    It was clear to me that there were environmental issues here so I asked the owner to describe her lifestyle. She went on to explain that Daisy went everywhere with her and that the only time she was alone was when she was teaching school. Even then she was close enough that she would come home during the lunch hour to let Daisy out. So at most Daisy was separated for no more than four hours at a time. Being that she had four roommates she spent very little of her free time at home other than to sleep. Most of the time was spent visiting friends and the like. When she was at home there was constant comings and goings of the four roommate's boyfriends as well as guests.

    Clearly for Daisy she lived in perpetual chaos. Constant change in the den was leading to high levels of anxiety. To underscore the point a new behavior had surfaced most recently where she would greet quests with hackles raised and animating barking. As with most evaluations we began with the basics, the sleep location. Daisy had been sleeping under the owner's bed with the bedroom door closed, clearly giving her an advantage where she could defend her pack (the owner) from a stealth position. With each and every night that passed with her successfully defending the den she was growing more sure of her position as Alpha. To make matters worse each morning she was being tossed a bowl of food as the owner was leaving for work allowing her to free feed during the day. All the more reinforcing her Alpha status. Clearly changing the sleep location to a kennel and instituting the Alpha feeding routine were needed as first steps, but even more important was to curb the aggression quickly.

The prescription was clear, for safety of the quests Daisy was not to be left off leash until the owner had Alpha well established. The key point was the owner had to have a method of control and ability to correct the canine when she started to act inappropriately. By using the proper equipment (leash and chain collar) the owner would be able to deliver the proper correction when the time came. The next ingredient would be cooperation. For the next twelve weeks she would have two types of guests, ones that would cooperate and ones that wouldn't. The cooperating guests would be instructed upon that arriving at the residence to completely ignore Daisy until she had been calm for at least five minutes. For non cooperating quests Daisy would need to be sequestered and not allowed access. The owner agreed and went on to say that in all three bite instances that the victims had upon entering the house went directly to Daisy to introduce themselves because they were supposedly "Dog" people. It seemed obvious that Daisy was simply trying to restore order in what was chaos by barking, growling, and sometimes nipping.

Both Sadie and Daisy had come from the same litter. Both dogs had ended in completely different places in development. Sadie a model canine citizen, Daisy on the edge. The most striking difference between the two dogs was how Daisy's owner handled play. As a young puppy Daisy's owner had allowed her to put her open mouth on hands during play (known as mouth jousting). In stark contrast Sadie's owners had never allowed it based on our program. Secondly, anytime Daisy had done something wrong she was punished (not corrected) and never given any positive praise. It was clear to see how the environment had created Daisy. Being that Daisy's owner was a school teacher it didn't take long to educate her on the program and process. I reminded her to be calm, confident, and consistent and that from this point forward she would be driving Ms. Daisy.

CASE STUDY: UNFORGIVABLE

Unfortunately not all case studies can have a happy ending. This case study is about a six-month-old, 90 lb., white German Shepherd Mix named Jake we worked with several years ago. Let me begin by stating that every possible medical test was given Jake to eliminate the possibility of any medical condition having caused a severe behavior disorder. The reason we have chosen to discuss Jake's case here is that the only unique characteristic is that the litter Jake came from never nursed the mother and was removed from the mother at the age of four weeks. We first came involved with Jake as the result of a pet sitting request.

Jake had been adopted by a fireman and nurse living in a nearby town. Jake had been afforded all the advantages a spoiled dog could imagine. She had the undivided attention of her owners in that there were no kids in the household. For the first few weeks Jake went everywhere with the couple. Daily trips away from home as well as weekly vacations up north. It was when the couple had decided that a trip to Hawaii was in order to beat the winter cold that they decided to engage a pet sitter to take care of Jake while they were away. A meeting was arranged where the pet sitter would meet Jake and go over any specifics during the planned four day vacation.

The meeting went pretty much according to plan except for the trepidation of the owners and them advising the pet sitter that if there were any problems to call the owner's brother and he would be able to help. This seemed sort of an odd thing to say but nothing too much out of the ordinary. So the couple and pet sitter parted with the first pet sitting day to be scheduled for the upcoming weekend. Now generally pet sitters watch your pet at your home, but don't stay there the entire twenty four hours. They come a few times a day to let the canine out, check water, feed, and medicate if necessary. As circumstance had it there would be only one visit from the pet sitter.

Fortunately the pet sitter had a companion along for the day for what was about to happen it was a fortunate event in deed. The pet sitter and companion entered the house and proceeded to go down into the finished basement where Jake was in her kennel. Nothing out of the ordinary yet Jake seemed happy to see them both and was anxious to get out of the kennel. The backyard was not fenced so the owners had put a dog tie-out-stake to which Jake could be attached and not run away. The pet sitter opened the kennel door in which Jake dashed immediately to the backdoor. The pet sitter opened the backdoor and attached Jake to the tie-out-stack without incident. What happened next was completely unexpected.

The pet sitter and companion remained inside preparing Jake's meal when they noticed some small pieces of paper blowing circularly in the wind. It didn't seem that important as pet sitter and companion opened the backdoor to go out and retrieve Jake from the tie-out-stack. But as the pet sitter approached Jake, she noticed that Jake was looking at the papers circling in the wind, when without provocation simply jumped up, grabbed a hold of the pet sitters arm clamped down and shook vigorously. Fortunately, for the pet sitter it was winter and with four layers of clothing the only puncture holes where in the outer three layers. As quickly as she had exploded she returned to wagging her tail as though nothing had happened. Absolutely terrified the pet sitter asked the companion to help get Jake out of the cold and back into the basement. Thinking fast the companion ran and got a couple of milk bones as a distraction. Having the distraction in hand the pair were able to get Jake back into the basement.

With Jake back in the basement and eating her food the pair noticed that every so often Jake would hesitate almost as if frozen. It seemed an odd behavior but neither could see any of the classic signs of a bite coming. None the less it concerned the pet sitter to the point that the fear of an attack was imminent due to the unpredictability of the canine. Jake was done eating making direct constant eye contact with the pet sitter. The pet sitter could see something wasn't right, so she quickly told her companion to get a tennis ball bounce it a couple of times throwing it into the kennel. The plan worked and Jake went in after the tennis ball while the companion closed and locked the kennel door.

Terrified the pet sitter called the emergency contact, the owner's brother and advised him of what had happened. His immediate comment was why hadn't they put the dog to sleep if they knew she was a biter? When asked he mentioned that he had been bit once and that his brother had been bit so badly that it required several stitches on his hand. His sister in law had been bit at least twice. The pet sitter informed the brother that no one from her company would be able to return because of the aggression. The brother said he understood and that he would take care of Jake for the rest of the vacation.

The owners came back from vacation and requested an evaluation on Jake. Having learned the history and circumstances surrounding the previous biting incidents we scheduled the evaluation. During the course of a normal evaluation Jake could not be provoked into biting. Actually based on the temperament assessment she would have been classified as having no possession aggression, human aggression, or dog-on-dog aggression. But the biting matter still remained, so we advised the owners to get a medical work up done that would eliminate any medical condition as the cause.

At the veterinary's office Jake started off the examination well with no incident or issue even during the drawing of blood samples. It was towards the end of the office visit that Jake tried to bit one of the vet assistants with no apparent provocation or warning signs. The owners were absolutely beside themselves they could not understand how Jake could go from "zero-to-bite". After consulting the veterinarian the owners decided that the best thing to do would be to euthanize Jake, she was a danger to herself and others. The owners decided one more day at home with them treating her to her favorite meals and toys would be the proper send off. Typically when owners take the canine back home they begin to get second thoughts, but what happened next solidified the decision.

The couple awoke that morning and gathered Jake out of her kennel and spoiled her with a sumptuous breakfast of eggs and bacon. Nothing seemed out of the ordinary, so the wife proceeded to sit down on the floor with Jake's head on her lap. She petted Jake for several minutes just as she had done several times before when all of sudden Jake leapt up and bit her in the face causing thirteen stitches. It was clear at that point that whatever was going on with Jake had gotten worse and the couple had no choice but to keep their three o'clock scheduled appointment with the veterinarian.

This is a rare case of "zero-to-bite" which I have only seen a half dozen or so times. I characterize these dogs as "Hard Wired Wrong" such as humans can have psychiatric disorders, but unfortunately these dogs are unforgivable and beyond rehabilitation.

CHAPTER 12
BASIC OBEDIENCE
CHOOSING THE RIGHT PROGRAM & TRAINER

Everyone likes a well-behaved dog, child, spouse, mongoose, Tasmanian devil, you name it. Not everyone has an appreciation for what it takes to have a truly well behaved dog or what I like to term "a well-mannered confident dog." Through basic obedience any dog owner can have a well-behaved dog that follows basic commands to the letter never having established an Alpha role with their dog. This is never more evident then with treat-based training. With this type of training dogs are rewarded for obeying commands with a treat. This training method can be somewhat ineffective especially when a car is bearing down on your dog and state the "Come" command without a treat in hand. We would all like to have our dogs follow our commands based out of love and respect that can only be established when we are in charge and viewed as Alphas.

We are often asked when starting Basic Obedience training if we can train children as well as dogs, unfortunately the answer is no. If I could have figured that one out I would have used it on raising my own children, wrote a book, and made a zillion dollars. I further explain that most dogs are very easy to train; it's the owners that we have a hard time training. In our methodology we don't even begin Basic Obedience training until we have covered how dog owners need to establish the Alpha leadership within their households. Layering Basic Obedience training on top of the Alpha principles provides dogs with a job and builds their confidence. Once the Alpha is established the dogs are ready to report for duty and begin the training program.

The most effective Basic Obedience training programs begin in the household. The training goes further to create this invisible bond and communication link between owner and dog. I made the mistake of not following this guideline some ten years ago or a point in time I like to refer to as before I was dog savvy. We had just gotten started working with Rescue and had four dogs in the household. Two of them were ours; the other two were long-term foster dogs, which eventually became ours. We became affectingly known as foster failures within the rescue community because we were not able to let go of our first two foster dogs. I can tell you these dogs ran the household. Any noise or knock on the door would start the dogs barking and driving me crazy. So being a good responsible dog owner I sent the dogs off to expensive boarding school for a few weeks. To my amazement and disappointment the dogs came back able to obey basic commands (using treats) but no better behaved around the household. After becoming dog savvy it became crystal clear that without establishing the Alpha the behavior was not going to improve.

There are many good training programs in the market and many not so good. The most effective training programs train you on how to train your dog. In other words you have the majority of leash time, not the professional trainer. Training sessions can be done in a group environment such as you might find at your local super pet store or an individualized one on one setting. Group sessions are great for socialization but sometimes lack the attention and focus some dog owners' need for unruly dogs. A one on one setting is great for focused training and quick results but lacks distractions that are helpful in getting your dog to focus on you. I have reviewed some training programs that have over twenty sessions defined with very detailed tasks defined for each session. That is ridiculous. Most of us have a hard enough time remembering our cell phone number on a daily basis let alone twenty some odd sessions with numerous tasks. One would have to walk around with the training manual while doing training sessions, not realistic. The best training programs have a half dozen sessions or less that build upon each other, such as basic obedience leading to intermediate obedience and so on. Each session has defined objectives and simple tasks. Once the objectives are met and tasks mastered that session is complete and you move onto the next session.

If you do decide to bring in a professional trainer into your home, do your homework and background checks. I always impress upon people that when you engage someone in doing professional services for you don't rely solely on references (chances are you will always get a good one). Don't hold too much stock in certifications or membership in professional associations and perform a criminal background check before letting them into your house to perform services. In other words, do your homework.

Over the years I have worked with several professional trainers, professional pet sitters, and rescue groups in developing effective Behavior Modification Plans and recommended Basic Obedience training programs for rescue canines. Here is an example of a Basic Obedience training program that is comprised of six lessons. The first four training lessons are conducted at the dog owners home (Den). The last two training lessons are conducting in a public setting. This blend of home and public setting provides the best results. For your convenience we have provided an outline of a Basic Obedience program with associated objectives and tasks.

JOHN KALEVI SIEVILA

TRAINING LESSON 1

(Perpetual Commands)

- ❑ Objective: Heel (Walk With Me, Stop With Me)
  - ➢ Starting Position → Left side, lead right hand waist high.
  - ➢ Begin → Start with a tap on left hand thigh; step forward with left foot stating "**Heel**".
  - ➢ Ending Position → At Stop, canine automatically assumes sit position (without command) left hand used for positive reinforcement or manipulation. End with **"Good Dog!"**

- ❑ Objective: Stay Command
  - ➢ Starting Position → Seated heel position, Left side, lead right hand waist high.
  - ➢ Begin → Step out with right foot with open right hand palm stating, "**Stay**".
  - ➢ Ending Position → Facing canine stating, "**Stay**" (3-5 minutes minimum). If canine moves from spot, step forward stating "No" and place back in exact position. End with **"Good Dog!"**

- ❑ Objective: Leash Corrections
  - ➢ Starting Position → Left side, lead right hand waist high. Chain collar must have some slack (2-3 inches).
  - ➢ Mild Correction → One quick snap from the end of the lead stating "No" followed immediately upon eye contact with positive reinforcement (e.g. "Good Boy!").
  - ➢ Stern Correction → 3 to 4 successive quick snaps from the end of the lead stating "No" followed immediately upon eye contact with positive reinforcement (e.g. "Good Boy!").
  - ➢ Severe Correction → Quick pull on end of lead lift canine's front paws off the ground stating, "No". Once the back legs have relaxed and the canine sits allow the front paws back on ground followed immediately upon eye contact with positive reinforcement (e.g. "Good Boy!").

- ❑ Objective: Home Work Sessions
  - ➢ Spend no more than 10 to 15 minutes a day on lessons.

THE DOG REDEEMERS

TRAINING LESSON 2

(Introduction to Single Use Commands)

- ❑ Objective: Down\Stay Command (Single Use Command)
  - ➢ Starting Position → Seated heel position, left side, lead right hand waist high.
  - ➢ Begin → Step out with right foot placing left hand firmly on canine's shoulders. Place right hand on end of chain collar and while pointing right index finger down state **"Down"** (State only once). Manipulate canine down by applying rocking pressure with left hand and pulling down with right hand (Leash hand).
  - ➢ Ending Position → Facing canine stating, **"Stay"** (3-5 minutes minimum). If canine moves from spot, step forward stating "No" and place back in exact position. End with **"Good Dog!"**

- ❑ Objective: Heel Around (Perpetual Command)
  - ➢ Starting Position → Facing canine (canine either in seated heel or down position) lead right hand waist high.
  - ➢ Begin → State **"Heel"** (multiple times) pulling canine to right hand side. As canine reached right hand side take 2 steps backward, then 2 steps forward working canine around back to assume a heel position on left hand side.
  - ➢ Ending Position → → At Stop, canine automatically assumes sit position (without command), left hand used for positive reinforcement or manipulation. End with **"Good Dog!"**

- ❑ Objective: Sit (Single Use Command)
  - ➢ Starting Position → Down heel position, Left side, lead right hand waist high.
  - ➢ Begin → State **"Sit"** (once only) taking a long step forward pulling on leash. Step back and manipulate canine into sit position with left hand.
  - ➢ Ending Position → Sit position at heel. End with **"Good Dog!"**

- ❑ Objective: Home Work Sessions
  - ➢ Spend no more than 10 to 15 minutes a day on lessons.

TRAINING LESSON 3

(Mixed Commands)

- ❑ Objective: Advanced Heel (Repetitive)
  - ➢ Assess behavior → Begin with left foot while canine is walking along left side stating "Heel", no pat on leg. A walk freely keeps pace with handler, no pulling on lead. Stop with canine in sitting position
- ❑ Objective: Down Command (Single use)
  - ➢ Assess behavior → Step out with right foot, place right hand on lead (near collar) pointing down with the right index finger stating "Down". Manipulate with left hand on dog's shoulder to place in down position.
- ❑ Objective: Down Stay From a Distance Command (Repetitive)
  - ➢ Assess behavior → Repetitious, open palm to face stating, "Stay" moving several feet away. Ensure canine doesn't move from location.
- ❑ Objective: Come Command (Single Use)
  - ➢ Assess behavior → From a down stay using a long lead clearly state "Come" while simultaneously using an extended right hand to side, clinched fist pulling to chest. Canine must stop directly in front and assume a sitting position.
- ❑ Session Review
  - ➢ Review results and Program guidelines.
- ❑ Objective: Home Work Sessions
  - ➢ Spend no more than 10 to 15 minutes a day on lessons.

THE DOG REDEEMERS

TRAINING LESSON 4

(Distance Commands)

- ☐ Objective: Down Stay From a Distance Command (Repetitive)
  - ➢ Assess behavior → Repetitious, open palm to face stating, "Stay" moving several feet away. Ensure canine doesn't move from location.
- ☐ Objective: Sit from a down stay. (Single Use)
  - ➢ Assess behavior →
  - ➢ One step forward, step back to get into sit position.
- ☐ Objective: Advanced Heel (Repetitive)
  - ➢ Assess behavior → Loop around back, assume heel position. Stop, should be in sitting position
- ☐ Objective: Come Command (Single Use)
  - ➢ Assess behavior → From a down stay using a long lead clearly state "Come" while simultaneously using an extended right hand to side, clinched fist pulling to chest. Canine must stop directly in front and assume sitting position.
- ☐ Bed/Kennel (Optional Command)
  - ➢ Assess behavior → Clearly state "Kennel up" or "To bed" while taking dog to location. Follow-up with "Stay", repeat 4-5 times daily to reinforce.
- ☐ Session Review
  - ➢ Review results and Program guidelines.
- ☐ Objective: Home Work Sessions
  - ➢ Spend no more than 10 to 15 minutes a day on lessons.

PROGRAM GUIDELINES DO(S) & DON'T(S)

Do(s)

- Ignore pawing, nudging, whining, especially first thing in the morning or when you walk in the door (5 minute rule). Alphas never acknowledge lower ranking members of the pack.

- Always go through exterior doorways, gates, and entry ways first. Alphas own the "den".

- At feeding time you eat first, allow your dogs to calm down (5 minute rule). Place the bowl down and don't allow them to eat until you've said, "OK". Alphas dictate which pack members eat in what order.

- If your dog perceives a threat by barking, get up acknowledge the threat and tell them good job. Alphas dispatch the threat.

- Do kennel your dog for the night, or place in another suitable location.

- Always make your dog move out of your way. This is a sign of respect for Alphas.

- Only pet your dog if he/she is sitting or lying down.

- Always take your dogs' "kills" (stolen articles or food) away from him.

Don't(s)

- Upon arriving don't acknowledge your dog by eye contact, verbal expression, or physical contact. Never give attention when your dog demands it.

- Never let your dog go first through doorways, gates, or hallways.

- Never leave food down for longer than 15 minutes at feeding time. Never interrupt your canine while eating.

- Never yell at your dog for barking at strangers, noises, etc. As a lower ranking pack member they are doing their job.

- Don't let you dog sleep on your bed, it sends them the signal they are equals.

- Never let your dog restrict your access to an area.

- Don't pet your dog unless it is in a submissive posture (e.g. sitting, lying down).

- Never let your dogs keep their "kills" (stolen articles or food). 1 chew toy allowed

THE DOG REDEEMERS

Do(s)	**Don't(s)**
• Always initiate games with your dog and win them (end up with the toy).	• Never play a game you can't win, don't give your dog the toy when the game is over.
• Always call your dogs' name for affection.	• Never call your dogs' name in anger.
• Always call your dog to you to give affection.	• Never walk over to your dog to give affection.
• Call their name once and run in the opposite direction if your dog "takes off".	• Never chase your dog yelling, "come!", if so their leading the hunt!
• Always reward your dog for completing an exercise well. End on a positive note!	• Never let the dog dictate when work is done.
• Give commands once, enforce any command you give.	• Never give commands over and over. Never give a command you can't enforce.

ESTABLISHING ALPHA

(12 Week Behavior Modification Program Guidelines)

1) **Sleep Location or Home Alone:** Sequestered in kennel or enclosed room. Canines are not allowed to sleep in bedrooms or on beds. Only Alphas have free roam of the den.

2) **Feeding Routine:**

a. Prepare canine food and prior to feeding them eat or drink something in front of canine (first 2 weeks).

b. Set the bowl down; if canine moves forward pick the bowl up. Continue this up and down motion until you can set the bowl on the floor and state, **"OK"** signaling it is acceptable for the canine to eat. Pick the bowls up within 15 minutes whether canine is finished eating or not.

3) **Leash Control:** While in the house the canine should have a chain collar on attached to a 6-foot leash. Remove leash when canine goes outside.

4) **Threshold Respect:** Alphas always enter and exit the den first. Your canines should not have free access to the outside via pet door or open door. When allowing the canine to enter the den (from outside or kennel) open the door, if they try to enter, close the door promptly. Continue opening and closing the door until you can leave the door open and state **"OK"**. When allowing the canine to exit the den, open the door and step out first. If the canine tries to follow close the door. Open and close the door until the canine waits for you to state **"OK"** before exiting.

5) **Furniture:** canines are not allowed on the furniture. If they attempt to get on state **"No"** with a simultaneous leach correction followed immediately upon eye contact with positive reinforcement (e.g. Good Dog!).

6) **Housebreaking:** Until you're confident that the canine is housebroken they must either be in the kennel or attached via lead to your belt loop. If the canine attempts to squat interrupt the activity by stating, "What are you doing???" pull the canine outside and when finished give positive praise (e.g. Good Dog!).

THE DOG REDEEMERS

7) **Chewing:** If the canine is chewing on something inappropriate substitute the item with their one chew item and the instant their teeth hit their chew item give them positive praise (e.g. Good Dog!). Never say "No" when caught.

8) **Toys:** The canine is allowed one action toy only. The action toy comes out when you decide it is time to play and gets put away when playtime is done. If using a tug toy or other physical game you must win every contest.

9) **Licking/Mouth-i-ness:** The canine is never allowed to lick your hands or feet more than twice in a row and is never allowed to put an open mount on any part of a human. Immediate leash correction is needed if this happens. Licking the face is OK and encouraged.

10) **Posturing:** The canine is only to be shown affection when in a submissive position (sitting or lying down). Intersecting with our physical space is not allowed unless we initiate. Bump the canine and don't show affection until the canine is in a submissive position.